D1450567

Writing From Personal Experience

Writing From Personal Experience

HOW TO TURN YOUR LIFE INTO SALABLE PROSE

NANCY DAVIDOFF KELTON

WRITER'S DIGEST BOOKS
CINCINNATI, OHIO

Other fine Writer's Digest Books are available from your local bookstore or direct from the publisher.

Visit our Web site at www.writersdigest.com for information on more resources for writers.

To receive a free weekly E-mail newsletter delivering tips and updates about writing and about Writer's Digest products, send an E-mail with the message "Subscribe Newsletter" to newsletter-request@writersdigest.com or register directly at our Web site at www.writersdigest.com.

04   03   02   01   00   5   4   3   2   1

Library of Congress has catalogued hard copy edition as follows:

Kelton, Nancy.
    Writing from personal experience / by Nancy Davidoff Kelton.
      p.   cm.
    Includes index.
    ISBN 0-89879-789-6 (hard cover)
    1. Authorship.
PN147.K423   1997
808'.02—dc21
ISBN 0-89879-972-4 (pbk.: alk. paper)   97-282
                                                                                          CIP

"My Lover Committed Suicide" appeared originally in *Cosmopolitan* (April 1986); excerpts have been reprinted by permission of the author, Carla Rae Merolla.

Edited by Jack Heffron
Production Edited by Jennifer Lepore
Cover Designed by Angela Lennert Wilcox

ABOUT THE AUTHOR

Nancy Davidoff Kelton's personal essays have regularly appeared in the *New York Times*, *Parents*, *New Woman*, *Newsday*, *Redbook* and numerous other publications. Her previous books include *Dating Is About Finding Someone So You Never Have to Date Again* and four biographies. She teaches writing at New York University and The New School for Social Research. She lives in New York City.

This book is dedicated to my students—
past, present and future.

ACKNOWLEDGMENTS

I want to thank Lee Bantle, Michele Bender, Holly Russell, Michele Cardella, Allan Ishac, Carla Rae Merolla and my other students for reminding me, as I wrote this book, of the things I've tried to teach them; all my Wednesday nighters for regularly sharing their best selves and making my work great fun; Stephanie von Hirschberg, Susan Lapinski, Tom McKean, Anne Pleshette Murphy, Wendy Schuman, Iris Sangiuliano, Jennifer Lepore, Judith Appelbaum, Florence Janovic and Craig N. Sellers for their invaluable suggestions, expertise, opinions, stories and support; Elizabeth Crow for these things too, plus her time and herself, and also for letting me sing; my agent Jean Naggar and everyone at the Jean V. Naggar Literary Agency; my parents, Max and Esther Davidoff, my staunchest supporters; my daughter, Emily, for tiptoeing around me and for eating the dinners we ordered in; and most of all, my editor Jack Heffron for being so very respectful, available and right on. To those I may have neglected to note, forgive me.

TABLE OF CONTENTS

INTRODUCTION

A few words about what you can expect from this book that you will not get from the *Cliffs Notes*.

Writing From Personal Experience is full of solid instruction. There are techniques, strategies and advice. From decades of turning my life into prose and having my students do the same, I have accumulated, in the eyes of the people who gave me this book contract, enough knowledge and hard-won truths to get you writing happily and regularly. Very, very soon.

This is *not* a standard instruction manual, though. It is partly that. But more. I will share—as I do in whatever I write—a heck of a lot of me.

I write from personal experience, so I'll be sharing mine. I look at life with my head slightly tilted so I will tilt as I talk to you.

Like my teaching, this book is quirky. A combination of how-to and how-I. Some chapters are instructional and long. Others are conversational and short. I teach and function best when personal. I don't relate to people or writing that's cold.

I have woven my stories in with the instructions. As a writer, teacher and friend, I know what it's like to face the blank page. I intend to encourage you.

This book will be like a "get-out-of-jail-free" card. It will help you express what is in your heart and mind long after you pass "go."

Expect to write. And I mean write. You can't just read or talk about it. There will be guidance throughout and exercises at the end of chapters. Do these exercises. Once. And again.

The more you write, the freer you become. I have been there. Done it. And know.

My passion and strength as a writing teacher is guiding students to their true selves. I will help you do that now too. My pointers, truths and stories are useless unless you write.

And write.

And write.

You need not read the chapters in order. They are self-contained. You can pick up the book and open it anywhere. For a nugget. An exercise. A lift.

I teach a course called Writing From Personal Experience. That is how I came to write this book. Another title I considered was *The Joy of Writing* because expressing ourselves freely is bliss. I also thought I might call it *Writing From Your Gut*. That's the only place from which to write.

In these pages I share everything I know about writing. And I suppose about living, too. They belong to the same cousins' club.

"So it sounds like your book is spiritual," a friend said, seeking a soundbite for this work.

Now, I find labelling irksome. It makes things too simplistic. Too easy. Too pat. Yet despite my annoyance I can and will say that "spiritual" is what this book is.

Expressing what's in our hearts and minds is a way of hanging out with our gods.

As long as I'm doing labels, I'd call this book "cyclical" too. Everything I say in here goes back to one or more of the following themes:

- Writing is about being courageous.
- It takes a willingness to let people see who we are.
- Talent plays just a tiny role.
- Determination is the key.

These are the gospel according to me. They have guided how I write and teach. If they leap out at you, so be it. Let them lead you to your truth.

My students say I'm tough on them. No argument from me. Tough in the sense that I mean business about being disciplined and hanging in. And about being authentic, saying what matters and being as economical as you can.

If you want to write, you can and will. Regularly and with joy. I will show you how to be disciplined. I will give you instructions to revise. I will help you find your voice so you will keep writing when you finish this book.

CHAPTER ONE

My Mystery

Be so true to thyself, as though be not false to others.
—*Francis Bacon*

$\mathcal{I}$n my last life in the 1970s I decided to write a mystery. I rarely read mysteries. I'm hardly a buff. But the personal essays I'd been regularly writing and less regularly selling were, in my accountant's words, a "hobby," a "loss" and a "bust." I thought I should write for success.

I outlined My Mystery in a notebook and described my characters on cards. I had everything I needed to tell My Exciting Tale.

Except excitement.

And joy.

And a compulsion to tell this tale. My body showed up at my desk each day, but my soul was in Lost-and-Found. The words I put on paper sounded like they came from a dying quail. I continued writing it anyway until I faced a problem too big to ignore.

I couldn't figure out who did it.

In *my* book.

That seemed like a clear enough signal that whodunits were simply "not me." I put it in a closet on my "not me" shelf next to my Aunt Sylvia's beaded flowers.

What to do next, I wasn't quite sure. I thought about pottery or ballet. Only I definitely didn't want to pot. Or plié. What I wanted to do was write.

But I wanted to write what *I* wanted to write. The stuff inside me. I'd hit false notes when I was not sincere. Writers, like actors, can't lie.

I went back to writing essays. Very personal and very "me." The kind I'd abandoned for a page-turning thriller when I tried to be someone else.

My purpose in telling you about My Mystery Detour is to let you know what it taught and brought me.

You must write for writing's own reward and for the intrinsic joy it brings. Achieving this bliss means following it, and writing what we feel. My Mystery came from over my eyebrows, not from the center of my gut. It wasn't sincere. It didn't gel. And I wasn't having fun.

Some writers find bliss when they make it up. Others tell it like is. The world according to Sue Grafton or Anne Rice is not the world according to me.

Or you.

Everyone has something special to say and a unique way of seeing and saying it. This individuality bubbles up when we allow it to happen and when we get out of our own way.

That doesn't mean tomorrow, though. Writing is a process. Our voices, subjects and selves come out in dribbles and spurts and rushes and streams. It takes trusting our guts. And lots of hard work.

The way to get better is by writing.

H.E.M.

I once had a student—I'll call her H.E.M.—who was a *H*igh-powered *E*xecutive in *M*arketing. When the class members introduced themselves at the first session, H.E.M. told us she was clever, organized and efficient. The reason she was taking the course was to write about the human condition.

As opposed to writing about an elm tree's condition, I wondered? Or about a sparrow's condition on Mars?

I asked, "Which human's condition do you want to write about first?"

H.E.M. then said, "My father's."

At the third session, she handed in an essay about him and their relationship. I read it to the class.

It was good. It had merit. Everyone was supportive. H.E.M. clearly had something to say.

We gave her constructive criticism and concrete suggestions on how to make it sing. With a tighter beginning, dramatized scenes and some dialogue, she would have a fully realized piece.

She never showed up again.

Where had H.E.M. gone? What had I done? I am Jewish. The fault must be mine.

A year later I ran into H.E.M. in the elevator of The New School for Social Research where I teach. I was on my way to my class. She was on her way to hers, a film class: Early Bergman to Truffaut.

"What happened to you?" I asked her.

"I enrolled in your class because I had read an essay in *Parents* you wrote about your father. I wanted you to tell me where I should send mine."

"There's a good chance I would have if you had made those revisions," I said.

"I didn't have the time," she said, looking at me like I had asked her to wash the ring around my bathtub and around the tubs of everyone in New York, "and the truth is I don't really like sitting in a room alone."

"Too bad," I told her. "You've got something there if you want to do the work."

"I thought my piece was fine," she said, then rushed off to Truffaut.

I have had many students like H.E.M. Slide right in. Then slide out. Think it's easy. Come for answers.

Never mind the labor.

I don't get to know them before they go bolting to "film."

But I am pretty sure they're not writers.

A writer likes to be alone in a room, and makes the time to get there. She writes because she can't not write. She's impelled from within to do it. She does it first and always for herself.

Not for outside approval.

"Do people become better writers from the act of writing or from getting more in touch with what they feel?" a student once asked me.

Loved that question!

"The way I see it," I told my student, "the two go hand in hand."

I am as giddy now about what words can do as I was at twenty-one. One student's main character is living inside me years after reading his novel. Another erstwhile student's essay about her brush with death is still haunting me today.

It wasn't *all* there in these students' first several drafts. Both revised. And revised. And revised.

FOUR TRUTHS ABOUT WRITING

Writing, like life, has few guarantees. I've arrived at four truths about it, though, from decades of writing and revising, and helping my students do the same.

One: Writing is hard work. Harder than buying manilla folders and "talking about writing" over latté, liquor or lunch. Writing is definitely harder than discussing the ideas of the novel you are going to write.

In the last two decades, I have heard the terrific ideas for novels from every cabdriver in New York.

Writing is not hard in the same way that dancing on one's toes and lifting a sofa are hard. We appreciate the difficulty of those labors just by watching dancers and lifters.

Writing is a deceptively difficult art. Time, patience, discipline, desire and perseverance are needed to reap its rewards. And even with all these things, the going can be tough.

I never tell my students it's easy. Quite often, it is anything but. Do it only if you really want to. There are easier ways to be miserable.

Now if you want to work, and I do mean work, here is my second truth: The rewards you will reap from writing are the greatest you could possibly know.

You have had a glimpse of the possibilities or you wouldn't have bought this book. The expansiveness and discoveries writing brings make you more conscious and alive.

Writing will bring you great freedom and power.

You get to hang out with your best self.

My third truth about writing is that if you do it regularly and consistently you definitely get better. I see it in my students' work. I see it in my own.

When I was a child and first saw Billie Jean King hitting the ball, I thought how easy and effortless good tennis playing is. All it takes is standing there, taking long and simple swings. Then I got on the court and klutzed around like I was having chronic spasms. I missed shot after shot, was nowhere near the ball, and began to understand.

Paring it down, making our efforts look smooth, is a lifelong process. When someone tells me they "hear" my voice in my writing, I know I am getting somewhere.

My fourth truth about writing: Nothing turns out as we expect it to. Nothing turns out as planned. *That's* the journey. *That's* the fun. Letting our unconscious take us along while we stay out of its way.

Juan Gris, the artist, said, "You are lost the instant you know what the results will be."

Isn't this true of all creating?

If you need to know where you will end up and the route to take, you best sign up instead for math. 2 + 2 is always 4. No surprises there.

Acclaimed author E.L. Doctorow beautifully compares writing to driving at night with headlights. You have a vague idea what is in front and where you might go, but you just see a little ahead.

I like that.

I agree.

Letting it happen and taking the ride. That's the joy of writing.

Exercise

1 Think about the things in your life—past and present—that are "you." Things like
- articles of clothing
- types of work
- types of people
- leisure-time pursuits
- academic subjects
- social gatherings (e.g., a weiner roast, the debutante's ball, a beer bash)
- movies
- music
- sports
- places to live
- houses
- furnishings
- vacations

Jot them down and write what it is that makes or made them a good fit.

Now jot down those things like Aunt Sylvia's beaded flowers that are or were "not you." Write why.

2 Think about your reading. About the books, stories and essays you like, quote from, recommend and read again and again.

List five favorites.

Write what it was about them that turned you on. Did they have common characteristics? If so, what were they?

Are you writing what you like to read or what you think you "should" write?

Think carefully about that. Write down your thoughts.

CHAPTER TWO

Sunday Near the Park With Me

Will you, won't you, will you, won't you, will you join the dance.

—*Lewis Carroll*

One Sunday each semester I teach an all-day writing workshop at New York University. Before the last one, there was a table in the lobby by the entrance with a self-serve continental breakfast for students and faculty. I had already eaten, but that did not stop me. I was propelled straight to the muffins and tea by two voices inside me, unmistakably my parents', saying, "Don't be a chump. It comes with."

I walked into the classroom. Several students were already there. The others straggled in with coffee, waried looks and pens. One woman had a paperbag full of crackers. She munched and rattled away. "Morning sickness," she announced to me and the twentysome people waiting to begin.

I introduced myself, spoke less than five minutes, then told them it was time to get going.

"Write about what brought you here," I said. "What made you register for the course? I don't care if it was a longtime yearning, a recent itch, a crisis or because the painting workshop was filled. What matters is the truth."

I went on. "Write what you felt and thought this past week, last night and this morning before coming. Write what you are feeling now."

Within seconds their pens were all moving.

Then I walked toward the door and told them I was going to the restroom. "I'll be back in a few minutes. Keep writing. Don't stop. And whatever you do, please don't copy."

I heard the titters I had hoped for from instructing them not to "cheat." My intent was to get them to relax and trust me. And to begin to trust themselves. Mostly though I wanted to remind and reassure them that what they each had to say was unique.

When I returned from the ladies' room, I wrote the following three sentences on the blackboard:

Listen to me.

Listen to yourself.

Write it down and keep the pen moving.

That was my overall plan for the workshop. And my overall plan here for you.

After ten minutes I told them to make notes about what else they might say on the topic and what else was bubbling up, then finish their sentence or thought. My stopping them while they were writing reminded me of the story about a music teacher who was lecturing her students about music. One day a marching band went by in the street below playing "When the Saints Go Marching In." The students rushed to the window and joyously joined in: singing, clapping, dancing and tapping.

"You are here for music," the teacher told them, "so go to your seats and be quiet."

"You're here to write," I reminded my class now. "So put

down your pens and listen."

The best way to learn how to write is by writing.

And like making music, there is no mystique.

Let go. Let it flow. Let your feelings out on the page.

That is what writing is. And it is not for a chosen few.

A WRITER'S FEARS

My students began to understand. Each had filled up more than one page. Writing is giving voice to our feelings and making discoveries about ourselves.

Several people shared what came out in that first exercise. We saw some common threads. They felt excited, free and expansive. They were also plagued with fears that

- They couldn't do it.
- They sounded dumb.
- No one could care what they had to say.
- They were too self-involved.
- Their families would disown them.
- They were going nuts.
- There was no point in doing it, because what they wrote was dreck.

Does any of this sound familiar? Are you plagued with some or all of these fears?

These insecurities are common to all writers. An integral part of the deal. As one writer confided in his journal: "My work is no good, I think—I'm desperately upset about it. Have no discipline anymore . . ."

Those were the words of John Steinbeck while he was writing *The Grapes of Wrath*. But he finished. He endured. How?

The way every writer does. He pushed past his insecurities and kept on moving his pen.

In later chapters, I will speak more about our internal critics and whoever gets in our way. For now, just send them on sabbatical and listen to yourself.

During the workshop, I gave my students several more exercises. They wrote. And they wrote. Until like the music teacher, I'd say stop.

Then we'd talk about writing. Then we'd stop talking. Then they would write some more.

They listened to me. Then to themselves. And kept putting more of themselves on the page.

Just as you will do.

Read my stories, truths and instructions here. Make sure you do the exercises, too.

You become a better writer by writing, and like the muffins and tea before my workshop, exercises "come with."

Exercise

1 Write what made you buy this book. If someone bought it for you, write who it was and why. If you borrowed it from the library and didn't buy it, write why. Remember: I'm not going to read what you are writing, so admit it if you're cheap.

2 Write five sentences on how you feel about your writing and about yourself as a writer. No one is going to see this. It's between you and you.

CHAPTER THREE

Every Day Between You and You

Good things—important things—take a long time to develop.
—My Mother

*I*t is nine A.M. on Sunday. I am about to write this section on writing every day. Running through my mind now is Woody Allen's wonderful line: 80 percent of life is about showing up.

I agree except when it comes to writing. Then the percentage increases. It is more like 97 percent.

Showing up not just in body, but with all that's inside of you, bringing everything Dorothy's buddies went looking for in Oz.

Talent may play a bit part. Desire and discipline are the keys. To be a writer, you must want to write. You must sit your behind down.

Every day, too. Like flossing and brushing. Make it a regular thing. Writing is writing. It is putting words down on paper. It's not saying, "If only I had time."

Write when you are inspired. And write when you are not. Inspiration is not always with us. And it doesn't come UPS.

It arrives when we aren't looking. Or when we are nowhere near our desks. And sometimes it comes *while* we are writing. What a joyous thing!

It shows up when we least expect it. Its hours are downright weird. If you wait for it to perch itself on your shoulder, you'll end up being a waiter.

And you may never write at all.

"There is no possibility, in me at least, of saying, 'I'll do it if I feel like it' . . . I must get my words down every day whether they are any good or not."

That was John Steinbeck. Same deal as yours and mine. He wasn't always sitting at his desk with a party hat on his head, happily writing sparkling prose.

He got there just the same.

You must too. You must show up. Sit down regularly and write.

WORK HABITS

I once had a student—a very good student—who went on to publishing fame. When she took my twelve-session class, she was not the best writer. She was certainly the most diligent. She showed up with manuscripts every week, not with lame excuses.

Someone asked her how she did it.

She said, "I pretend I am going to iron."

Iron?

My student went on. "You have to drag out the ironing board and set it up. Then you take out the iron and put it on steam or steam/spray or spray/steam. Then you plug it into the outlet, put the wrinkled shirt on the table and start ironing away.

"It's a pain to set up. It's a drag to get yourself there, but once you are at it and your hand is moving, you just keep ironing and ironing."

Or writing. And writing. And writing.

It doesn't matter when you sit down to write. The important thing is to carve out time.

I know one writer who works in the afternoon. He has an office job until noon. I know another writer who works late at night after she puts her children to bed. Still another—an attorney—writes weekends and most evenings. By adhering to this schedule, he wrote a novel that was published last year, and he is now finishing up his second.

I prefer writing in the morning. As early as possible, too. I am closer to my dreams, my unconscious and my true self then. My superego has not yet kicked in.

Daily living requires role-playing. It clutters and clogs our minds. I see it and say it fresher before I put on my armor and mask.

On some days I am at it by six or seven. I have coffee and whatever, then write. On other days, it takes longer because I get in my own way. I think of the rituals of other writers. They meditate. Drink more coffee. Take walks.

I usually do all three.

Next I pluck an eyebrow or two, water my plants and water them some more. Then I call the bank to get my balance. I call my friend Cindy to get the dirt. When I run out of humans to chat up and pester, I leave monologues on friends' machines.

Finally, finally, after I've exhausted every means of procrastination I know, I sit down to face the blank screen and myself.

Not always at dawn, but I get there.

I start to write and sometimes it flows. That's my favorite kind of high. The rewards are amazing. It's like when you ski down a patch of moguls and hit them all just right.

But on too many days it isn't happening. It all comes out like mush. I sound dumb. And get dumber.

Will everyone find out I'm a fraud?

Sometimes on these days from hell, I start rolling at the end.

Then I can't wait until the next morning to get to it again. But on other days, my writing is ca-ca when I start. And ca-ca when I end.

"Some days are like that. Even in Australia," says Alexander in Judith Viorst's children's book *Alexander and the Terrible, Horrible, No Good, Very Bad Day.*

And some days are like that for those of us who express what is in our hearts and minds. All creative people have ebbs and flows and highs and lows.

Not every day is great.

Put that sentence on an index card and tack it up by your desk along with this next one by W. Somerset Maugham:

Only a mediocre writer is always at his best.

Now give yourself the latitude to write ca-ca and to have less-than-terrific days.

HOW TO CARVE OUT TIME

Start with a half hour a day. Do nothing else then, but write. You can use an exercise from this book or work on something of your own. Keep the words coming for the entire half hour no matter how clunky they sound.

Staring at your thighs doesn't count.

Neither does answering the phone. If it rings during that half hour, do not, for any reason, pick it up.

Making that half hour matter means carving out the time. Give up a half hour elsewhere. Make a shift in your routine. Here are ten viable suggestions:

- Skip your second cup of coffee.
- Don't stay on the phone.
- Wake up a half hour earlier.
- Don't take the whole lunch hour for lunch.
- Order in dinner instead of cooking it.

- Let someone else in the house do the dishes.
- Let someone else in the house do the wash.
- Skip the daily crossword puzzle.
- Don't read the entire newspaper.
- Take less luxurious baths.

And here is one. It is a course requirement whether it becomes writing time or not:

Skip the TV sitcom and all other shows that turn you into a passive lump.

HOW TO KEEP GOING

One technique I often use and highly recommend is to stop when you are cooking rather than writing until you are dry. This sounds like ending a relationship that's working. It's not. It keeps one very alive. When I give in-class exercises to students, I stop them when they are moving their pens. I want them to want to continue after they walk out the door.

Exercise

Think of a place in your life—past or present—that was special. Where you felt very safe and comfortable.

It can be inside or out. In a home—yours or someone else's—or somewhere you went summers or on vacations.

It can be standing over an ironing board.

Write about this place. Describe it, how you felt there and what made it so great.

Go to that place in your imagination during your writing time.

CHAPTER FOUR

Just Do It, Man! Just Do It!

Genius is 1 percent inspiration and 99 percent perspiration.
—*Thomas Edison*

One of the most common questions people ask me is, "Can you teach someone to write?" This is a compli- cated question—more complicated than the asker thinks. I have three answers.

ANSWER NUMBER ONE

The first answer is, "No, but I can teach someone to rewrite."

If you want to write, not "be a writer," rewriting is a big part of the deal. Unlike my student H.E.M., you can't write one draft then take a course in "Film."

My longtime students are first-rate writers. Their work is masterful and I tell them. That word never passed my lips when they showed up five years and six drafts ago. They keep digging and probing. They open up to the process. To me. And to themselves.

They write and rewrite, chiseling away and paring it down to its essence.

It means persevering. It's about commitment. I am not the Famous Writers' School. My student Michele sold a piece to the *New York Times*. What they bought was her fourteenth revision.

She was a willing apprentice.

At a party over crabmeat canapés, a cardiologist cornered me with His Plan. He had a terrific idea for a novel and thought he'd ask the hospital for a three-month leave. Although he'd never written much other than prescriptions for nitroglycerin, he thought he'd write and finish it in my workshop, then I could send it to my agent.

"Fine," I said. "Then when you go back to work, I'll take three months off so I can do coronary transplants."

There are no easy rides or free professions. Everyone pays dues.

It is a lifelong process paring it down and writing from our true selves. Michelangelo did not sculpt The David in a day. He spent years breathing life into marble.

I am a very inspired teacher for students who revise.

ANSWER NUMBER TWO

My second answer to "Can I teach writing?" is, "Some technique, but that's just a small part. Mostly, I give space and guide."

That means guiding someone to her true self. And providing the space to get there.

Several people live within each of us. The child and critical parent are two. The child is Our Creativity. The one bursting to tell it. She's excited. Energetic. Alive.

The parent stands over her with a pickle face. It's Here Come The Judge. And worse. She slaps the child's hand as those truths tumble out, screaming, "How could you? How could you? How could you?"

As a teacher, I help students shut the parent's voice up so the child can hear her own. Then she is free to hang out with the gods and write her truth.

According to children's book writer and illustrator Maurice Sendak, the child is the only part to be trusted.

ANSWER NUMBER THREE

My third answer is, "Yes. If the someone shows up emotionally and really wants to write."

There must be *passion*. A spark. An inner light. It has got to be there. Burning. It is the fuel that propels the engine. If there is no passion, I can't instill it. You're better off at "Missing Persons."

I have a student. I'll call her Ruth. She took my class several years ago and wrote a few short stories. It was her first foray into fiction. Her efforts were good, but far from polished. Clearly, she had potential.

At the end of the semester, she came and thanked me for the encouragement, then told me she had taken my class for her job and needed a letter of confirmation.

I wrote the letter. That was it. She didn't come back the next term. Had writing been a lark for her? There was nothing, of course, I could do.

A year later, I ran into her in midtown Manhattan. We said "hello" and for several seconds, she seemed to drift off somewhere, then a spark appeared in her eyes.

"Something's going on with me," she said, her everyday office eyes grew brighter. "Is there room for me in your group?"

There was. Ruth joined my group and began a novel. It had promise. It was good. It got better. And now four years and five revisions later, it is beautiful and compelling. The mix of narrative voice, description, dialogue, character, plot development and rumination hang in perfect balance. The protagonist is more alive and engaging than many people I know.

Week after week, year after year, Ruth shows up at class with chapters. And every morning in between, she shows up at her desk.

"What's the secret?" asked another member of the group. His internal critic had moved in.

"I want to write," Ruth told him. "If there is something inside of you that you wish to say, *that* is reason enough to say it."

"Doesn't it ever feel hard?"

"God yes!" Ruth said. "But I do it, man. I just do it."

If you want to write—really write—nothing anyone can say will stop you. So be courageous. Let it come out your way. No one starts out masterful.

There's plenty of time for revisions.

Send your inner critic on sabbatical and just do it, man. Just do it.

Exercise

1 List three reasons (or people) that have kept you from "just doing it." Elaborate on each.

2 Write about a person who understands you and touches you.

CHAPTER FIVE

Writers in Training

*To keep the body in good health is a duty. . . . Otherwise
we shall not be able to keep our mind strong and clear.*

—Buddha

*I*t is 3:45 on Friday afternoon. My Body Sculpt Class is at
5:00. I put on my leotard and tights early this morning. I
have been ready to squat since dawn.

After Body Sculpt, I'll take an aerobic class or use the station-
ary bike. Then, even though I pride myself on being a devoted
teacher, an intensely social creature and truly loyal friend, I will
spend the evening *not* attending either an erstwhile student's
reading of a work-in-progress or a party to which I had RSVP'd
"Yes."

Instead I will go home and get into my new Robertson Davies
novel, a hot tub, my old red flannel bathrobe and myself, and
leave my Reeboks and guilt at the door.

So what does this all have to do with our writing?

Who cares when I read or sweat?

What I am doing now and for the rest of this day has three
commonsense truths for you.

SNEAK IN TIME

A good time to write is when you hadn't planned to write, but when you are about to go out or do something else. I wrote this morning as usual. I didn't plan to write now. It started bubbling up a half hour ago while I was about to return a call.

Instead I returned to you.

I love writing *when and what* I had no expectation to write. It is like reading comic books in the bunk after lights out. Or passing notes from row one to row five and back, because the substitute teacher is on the moon.

Since this is not my real writing time and this section did not figure into the book, it's no big deal if nothing happens. The pressure is clearly off.

Often when I am cooking or reheating, I get an idea, a flash, a glimmer. Fortunately, my writing space is ten feet from my kitchen. Dinner's late. Or burned.

If something hits you when you don't seem to be writing or when you "should" be doing something else, let the words flow and the ideas come pouring out.

It's like sex that is not required.

A hoot when you can sneak it in.

GIVE YOUR SOUL DAILY ATTENTION

Staying focused means nurturing yourself and saying no to "shoulds" and to role-playing. That is why I am "closed" tonight. That is why I'm not partying. It took me years to find solitude for activities that weren't "my writing."

With full-time work and a full-time child, I majored and minored in giving.

Writing demands a full tank. And more. I am learning to say "no" to what's depleting and unnourishing. I am learning to fill my own well.

Here is a list of what is nourishing:

- deep breathing
- lots of solitude
- lots of laughs
- friends who understand writing and deadlines
- friends who understand you
- a good hairstylist
- good books
- more solitude
- more laughs
- deeper breathing
- the avoidance of people and activities that are toxic, draining or take you away from yourself
- lots of sleep
- good food
- lots of exercise

HAVE A HEALTHY BODY

My best childhood friend's older brother—a gym teacher now— used to make us tremble.

"If I ever catch you smoking," he told us, "you'll eat the cigarettes lit."

"Sissies," he called out from his bedroom window as we were getting into the backseat of their mother's car to go shopping on Hertel Avenue. "If you had any sense in your little peabrains, you would put on your sneakers and walk."

As our regular Saturday baby-sitter, he let us watch *Oh Susanna* through *Your Hit Parade*, but at eleven it was lights out or else.

"If I hear one word from your room then, I'll come in and sit on your heads."

He did not crush our heads or shove our lit cigarettes down our throats. We had enough sense in our little peabrains to talk and smoke at my house.

Behind his back, we laughed at him. We called him Bully and Creep.

Today I would probably marry him.

I do not smoke. I walk everywhere. I'm asleep after *Your Hit Parade* or before. I like putting my squatting clothes on at dawn.

When I started writing my last book, I became a "serious worker outter." Not just because my forty-something body needed toning. I really wanted to feel good.

I believed in the mind/body connection long before the phrase was "in." For one to work well, they must both be in shape. Otherwise, there is no deal.

Our bodies, like our souls and spirits, require daily attention.

That is why when I shut off my computer, I get myself to the gym. I see and say it better when I am feeling good.

My body is hardly an athlete's. My routine, though, comes pretty close.

Mentally, spiritually and aerobically, I think it is important to be fit.

Eat well. Stay fit. Avoid what is toxic to your body and soul.

If you want to write, you must not just show up, but show up feeling good. Your mind, soul and body all work together. Make sure they are in excellent health.

Exercise

Exercise regularly.

CHAPTER SIX

Whole Days Can Be Trouble

The value of life lies not in the length of days, but in the use we make of them: A man may live long yet live very little. Satisfaction in life depends not on the number of years, but on your will.

—*Michael de Montaigne*

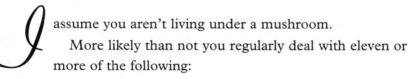 assume you aren't living under a mushroom.

More likely than not you regularly deal with eleven or more of the following:

- a job
- a family
- problems with the above
- laundry
- stains
- unwanted rodents
- unwanted houseguests
- an ex

- a cheap ex
- PMS
- PTA
- nosy neighbors
- noisy neighbors
- noisy radiators
- a noisy refrigerator
- several appliances that need fixing
- no one in the house to fix them
- a lawn that needs cutting
- superfluous hair that needs removing
- carpools
- car problems
- dates
- really awful dates
- weeds
- a checkbook that must be balanced
- business meetings
- allergies
- bunions
- a chiropractor
- in-laws
- the gym

Lots of big-time responsibilities and obligations. Many on-going chores. Chronic conditions and nudgy people putting ripples in our routines.

With such busy, busy lives, how can we manage to write?

We make the time. We carve it out. Every committed writer does.

In my twenties, I spent five days a week as an elementary schoolteacher of "acting out" students and seven days a week as a wife. I cooked dinner and wrote lesson plans most evenings. I had migraines by three o'clock most days.

An older, more established writer who had three kids, a

husband, a full-time job and a regular magazine column advised me to treat my writing as if it were illicit sex.

OK.

I snuck it in whenever I could between my "oughts" and "chores" and "shoulds." I wrote on weekends, after school or instead of my lunch or "prep." I savored my moments. I relished the time. It was mine. And nobody else's.

Still, I harbored the dream of having whole days to write when I stood in front of my classroom listening to my most serious "behavioral problem" bang incessantly on his desk. I made the dream come true. I took a leave from teaching to write full time.

It took me longer each morning to walk to the desk in my bedroom than it took to get to my elementary school by bus. First I'd put on a muumuu. Then I would change to jeans, then to sweats. Then I would sit over three cups of coffee. Then I'd stand over my one spider plant. I'd water it. And water it. And water it some more. Then I'd get paper towels to wipe the enormous puddle I had made on my parquet floor.

Because I had whole days, I would talk on the phone. Then I would go out and talk to the butcher. Sometimes I spent the entire morning talking to anyone who would listen.

When I had whole days to write, I wrote a whole lot less.

I missed the structure. The stimulation. My life outside my home. I also missed the public school, which provided me with fodder. I went back as a sub, worked in numerous schools and encountered a wider range of students. I now had children who summered in Woodstock as well as those who wintered in jail. My well was filling up again. I wrote as much as I had before.

I turn a deaf ear to people who say they can't write because they don't have the time. It is never the reason. The most prolific writers I know have full, demanding lives.

My advice: Don't quit your day job.

And don't quit your life.

If you are not or need not be gainfully employed, make sure

you are gainfully something else.

Don't move into a flotation tank. Or to Disney World or a spa. Volunteer, take classes, pursue hobbies, see friends, do community service, lend the elderly a helping hand.

Establish a routine in which you alternately go out and go within. One that connects you to something larger than yourself and enables you to *give*.

THREE SAYINGS

Whole days can be trouble. So is having too much time. Commitments, responsibilites, relationships and problems are really where it is at. They enhance and expand our worlds. They lead us toward our best selves.

They give us structure and something about which to write. So much of my life as a teacher and a full-time single mother has found its way into print.

Here are three sayings—one familiar and two new—you can put on three-by-five cards and tack up on the wall:

Give a busy person a job and you can be sure it will get done.

Give a person a whole day to write and she'll overwater one pathetic plant and find nineteen other ways to blow it.

Give a writer a busy, full life and she will find time to commit it to paper.

Exercise

1 Write about one weekday and one weekend day in your past or present life that brought you pleasure. Write why.

2 Write about one weekday and one weekend day that brought you grief. Write why.

Remember: No one in your life will see this.

CHAPTER SEVEN

Say No/Say Later

We learn to do something by doing it. There is no other way.
—*John Holt*

Because I work at home all day, I like to eat breakfast out. The coffee shop at my corner opens at six A.M. I often arrive before the bagels.

I once imagined the owner and waiters thought I was a lady of the night. But they regularly see me in sweats and big T-shirts, which may or may not have spots. I write on napkins and have a zoned-out look, so they must assume I am not in sales.

Whatever they or anyone else assumes about my clothes, behavior or work doesn't matter to me. It took years to break the "good girl" rules. To let my writing take center stage.

When I am at my desk working, I do not pick up the phone. Schmoozing is my addiction so like those in AA, OA and NA, I have learned how to "just say no."

I want to write. I'm impelled to write. It's got to be first things first.

If you want to write—really write—you must also make a commitment.

This is particularly hard for women with children. Young ones need shoes, a ride, a bandage or undivided attention. Teenagers need an outlet for their hostility. They blast us out of our solitude and space with their belligerence and music. With a family's demands, our time is hardly our own. All the more reason to make it. It is quite possible—and probably healthier—to carve out that half hour.

When my daughter was an infant, I had a sitter several mornings a week. I took my legal pads and pen and wrote at the library. When I was getting divorced, I didn't stop writing despite my daughter's more profound needs. There was no way I could be there for her unless I was there for me.

As a single mother with attorneys and dates, I had what to write about. I didn't have to look far. The worse it got, the better I wrote. Lucky me, for the pain.

The good news: Nothing bad happens to a writer.

Your experiences and struggles are a gold mine of material. Don't let them interfere.

Erma Bombeck, may she rest in peace, was an admitted workaholic. She didn't start out with a room of her own. She was an Ohio housewife and mother. Right before her fortieth birthday, after the last of her three children started school, she was determined to change her life. She later recalled that time in a published interview.

> . . . I used to sit at the kitchen window, year after year, watching women like Ruth Gordon, Anne Morrow Lindbergh and Golda Meir carving out their careers. I decided that it wasn't fulfilling to clean chrome faucets with a toothbrush. At 37, I decided it was my time to strike out.

Her time. Bombeck didn't just do the laundry and turn it into a piece. No. She was up at 6:00 every morning and at her keyboard by 8:30. She sat in her room with door closed until noon.

"I don't talk on the phone or come out of my thoughts for any-body." After lunch and a little nap, she resumed writing again.

> People tell me they want to write but that they have this house and those three kids and that carpool and . . . hey . . . the priority has to be *this*, right at the top.
>
> When my children were little and they'd come home from school wanting something, I'd simply have to tell them flat out, "Later". . . the writing always came first.

Get it?

Say "later" or "no" to anything that comes between you and your writing. You might feel a wee bit guilty. You may bewilder or anger those who want your time.

Eventually they will understand. If not, write anyway.

Here is the next exercise. Do it. It "comes with."

Exercise

Think about chores and people who get or have gotten in your way.

Jot who or what they are and how they have affected you.

Write about an incident or experience using one of the above that left a profound mark.

CHAPTER EIGHT

Writing Is Acting on Paper

. . . to be nobody but yourself in a world which is doing its best, night and day, to make you everybody else—means the hardest battle which any human being can fight, and never stop fighting.

—*e.e. cummings*

I took the same writing class several times and not because I flunked. I will devote later chapters to classes and what to expect from them. This is about something I learned from mine.

Our first assignment was a two-page character sketch of someone who touched our lives. The instructor said to use dramatic scenes and dialogue to capture the person's essence.

As he was speaking, my then mother-in-law flashed into my mind wearing her full-length mink. Her last visit had turned me into a quivering adolescent. I was still recovering.

And still putting my furniture, pictures and knickknacks back where they belonged. Upon her arrival while I was getting drinks in the kitchen, she rearranged my entire living room.

I relived that scene on paper. I then relived another as strongly etched out in my mind.

It had taken place the month before at her house one Sunday evening. My then-husband and father-in-law, both serious football nuts, had been glued to an enthralling Giants game. Admittedly so enthralling that even I kept checking in. When there were three minutes left of this enthralling game, my mother-in-law, may she rest in peace, put the brisket on the table and told us to come in.

I got up. They continued watching. She said, "Dinner's on," again. When they didn't budge, I could feel it coming. It was a scene they had played many times.

She charged into the den, turned the Giants game off, screaming again that dinner was ready, demanding they come to the table *now*.

She flew into a rage. So did they. The three of them went apeshit. She yelled until they succumbed. We somehow got to the table. Neither my husband nor his father said a single word. Somehow I managed to eat the brisket. Probably because it was good, but in my entire life I have never been so uncomfortable at the dinner table.

That Sunday and the one when she became my interior decorator formed the centerpiece of my character sketch. My teacher thought it worked well. "You showed who she was through vivid scenes," he wrote, "without using the word 'controlling.'"

The subject of my second character sketch was a man whom I knew at work. We had never been involved romantically. We weren't related through marriage or blood. He was pleasant enough to work with, but didn't stir me up inside.

That was the problem.

"Pleasant" makes lousy copy. Good writing is deeply felt.

What came out of me in describing him was a flurry of adjectives. From my head, not from my heart. It didn't fly like my last sketch had. My teacher said there was too much telling. He called it "uninteresting" and "flat."

Several years later when I took the same class again, I wrote about a boyfriend with whom I had recently broken up. It came out of me easily. The feelings were right there. The love. The loss. The pain.

My teacher thought this sketch had depth and that I brought the guy to life. How could I not? He was alive for me. He had really gotten my kishkas.

My teacher also thought I had just scratched the surface. He assumed I had more to say and suggested I flesh out the sketch further. I worked on it more that semester and after, then eventually sold it as an essay to *New Woman*.

WRITE FROM THE HEART

I wasn't finished with that boyfriend. Not in my feelings or on the page. I mined "us" and "him" from different perspectives. For years he showed up in my work.

There is simply no end to what a writer has to say about passion and about love.

Writing, in some ways, is like love: You cannot fake it. You have got to feel it. *It has got to come from your heart.*

Writing is like acting, too. If you don't feel what you are putting on paper, it simply will not ring true.

Ben Johnson, the late actor, had been a double and a stunt man for John Wayne and Henry Fonda when the director John Ford found him and began casting him in leading roles. Ford was truly taken with Johnson's work. He called him many amazing things including "the most photogenic, natural actor in town" (*Times*, obituary, April 9, 1996, p. B8). Here is what Ben Johnson said in response:

If Mr. Ford says I'm an actor, I reckon I am. But Lord help me if they ever ask me to do anything except be myself.

Lord, help any writer, too, who tries to be someone other than himself on the page.

Exercise

Write a two-page character sketch of a person who has really gotten under your skin. Use dramatic scenes. *Show* him or her in action. Don't *tell* us what the person was like.

Make sure the person you bring to life is a whole lot more than "pleasant."

CHAPTER NINE

It's Not About the Niña or the Pinta

Mastery is an accumulated strength, not dependent on imme-diate outer conditions or the approval of others.

—Gail Sheehy

Your next exercise—which is my students' first—is a two-page open letter to a person in your life sharing something you want to say. It can be unfinished business. Or the deepest longings of your heart. By "open," I mean you won't mail it. It is all between you and you. That way you can *really* be "open" and totally honest with yourself.

The letter must be genuine. The emotions must be real.

The reason I assign this and not a character sketch as a first class assignment is that in a letter it is often easier to get rolling. Easy to be free. And we all have significant or not-so-significant people in our lives to whom we have what to say.

Some people have or have had mothers whom they are dying to blame for *every big and little way she has brought them misery.*

The first two semesters of assigning open letters, I was flooded with this theme and its variations:

> Dear Mom,
> My life is a mess. I can't find work. Or relate to human beings. It's all your fault. I'm miserable and lonely. You robbed my self-esteem.

So I am telling you what I began telling students the third semester: Write a letter to someone you know well sharing your feelings and/or getting something off your chest. It can be to a spouse, lover, ex, friend, someone at work or school or to any member of your family: son, daughter, sibling, cousin, aunt, uncle, nephew, niece or father.

It cannot be to your mother blaming her for what went wrong.

GETTING REAL

I had a student, I will call him Stu. No, he did not write to his mom. But he also did not write to someone he knew well. Or to anyone on this planet.

He wrote to Christopher Columbus.

The students in my beginning classes aren't required to read their work aloud. They only do so if they wish.

Stu came in beaming on open-letter night. He wanted to read first. He announced that his letter was to Columbus. The other students laughed. Then he began "Dear Chris" and paused. He still got several laughs.

In the first part of the letter, he thanked Dear Chris for his voyage. And for putting us (heh heh) in our place. He then went on speculating about what would and would not have happened if Chris had taken the Niña, the Pinta and the Santa Maria on a different route. Where would we be today?

Stu finished reading and looked around the room grinning. He was the only one.

"Let's discuss it," I said to the class.

One student thought the idea was funny. Someone else said it was "cute." Another felt the opening paragraph was clever, but then it lost its steam.

Stu, still smiling, turned to me, wanting me to say, "It's great." I didn't.

I also didn't say what was going through my mind:

1. That if Columbus had not gotten here in 1492, I would not be listening to this dumb letter.
2. That Stu must have grown up being told he was funny. And the person who probably told him was his mother. And if he wanted to write one of those not-so-nice letters to her now, it would be deserving and I would let him.

Mostly, though, I was thinking about how much Stu had ticked me off for trying to be "cute" and not fulfilling the assignment. The letter was to be someone he knew well.

In a gentle, indirect, roundabout way, I told Stu to "get real."

"You obviously have a sense of humor," I said, "and it will emerge quite naturally if you let it, but now I want you to do the assignment I gave. For next week, write a letter to someone you know, saying something you really feel. Don't try to be funny. OK?"

He nodded.

I didn't know if it was OK or not. I don't reach every student. He might have been thinking what H.E.M. (the student I discussed earlier, who wanted to write about "the human condition") had of me: What does she know?

The next week Stu came with a new letter. It was to his fourteen-year-old daughter. He had just seen her for the first time in five years, which was when he left her mother.

He wrote about not being part of her life and about how the divorce and his selfishness cost him, revealing how frightened and excited he had been before their recent evening together and how truly beautiful she had become. He hoped she might begin to forgive him, and renew their relationship as well.

Everyone was quiet when Stu finished reading. Except for me. I was sobbing away.

"It's wonderful," someone told him.

The entire class agreed.

This time I simply nodded when he looked in my direction. I love when my students "get real."

Exercise

Write your two-page open letter now to someone who has touched your life, not to Columbus or Magellan.

Say the stuff that matters most to you.

Don't try to be funny. Just be.

CHAPTER TEN

Surprise! Surprise!

Writers, by their nature, spend their time thinking about,
wondering about, delving into, trying to understand the very
things that the rest of the world doesn't like to think about.

—Harry Crews

My "Dear Chris" student traveled far from Columbus to his daughter. In his second letter, he was not pretending. It came straight from his heart.

There is no other place from which to write.

YOUR OPEN LETTERS

So let's discuss your open letters now:

- To whom did you write or are you writing now?
- What is coming out on the page?
- Is what you are writing surprising you?
- How?

There is no one way to answer the above four questions. There is no one way to write.

If a person immediately came to mind to whom you wanted

to write, you probably have a lot to say. I hope you are getting it out.

Remember: The person is never going to see the letter. It is all between you and you.

If you thought of several people, write to the one for whom you have the strongest feelings; the one most under your skin. How do you know who that is? Listen to what's bubbling up.

Don't be afraid. Don't second-guess yourself. Let your gut now be your guide.

You can write those other letters after. You can also change your mind. To whomever you write and whatever the emotions, let the words and feelings flow.

Your letters will probably surprise you. And lead you where you've only subliminally been. To joy, anger, love, regret, remorse, loss, longing, lust, wistfulness and pain.

I trust you got to one or more.

They are all inside of us.

Open letters are terrific exercises. They help us begin to pull things out. When my students finish this assignment, they typically say two things: "I didn't know I felt that way" and "I had an idea what I wanted to say, but was surprised by where I went."

So I am not surprised if you are surprised.

That *is* one of the things that happens.

Isn't that why we write? To discover what we are feeling. To sort the whole thing out.

These letters may inspire other letters. Or essays or longer works. If you find your letters lead to more, let the "more" just happen.

One student wrote her open letter to a long-lost childhood friend. It inspired her to make up a story about two very different girls. She is happily working on a young adult novel she is calling

Dear Ellie, Dear Maude.

Feelings give way to more feelings. Keep at it. They will keep bubbling up. With your open letters and all other writing, do not be afraid.

Exercise

Write another open letter, letting go even more.

CHAPTER ELEVEN

The "What to Bring" List

Sorrow and silence are strong, and patient endurance
Godlike.

—Henry Wadsworth Longfellow

From ages nine to thirteen, I spent eight weeks each summer at Camp Tamakwa in Algonquin Park, Ontario. It was a popular overnight camp for little Jewish princesses and princes who came from Detroit, Toronto, Buffalo (my hometown) and new money.

The girls had "outfits." Their sweaters were cashmere. They primped more than they canoed. The boys had attitudes. They were cocky and fast.

Everyone made out in the boathouse.

This was not a crowd into which I easily fit. I didn't primp. Or neck. But I had a grand old time at Tamakwa, anyway, thanks to Uncle Lou.

The owner's energy and spirit dominated daily from flag-raising through taps. He had them in abundance. And insisted we did too.

Each May he sent us a "What to Bring" list divided into five sections: Clothing, Bedding, Miscellaneous, Optional, and first and foremost: Yourself. Under Yourself was the following:

1. Sense of humor
2. Desire to learn
3. Willingness to share

These made all the difference at Tamakwa. And everywhere I have taken them since. I could not write without them. And neither, I believe, can you. So along with passion, truthfulness, discipline, which we have already discussed, bring . . .

A SENSE OF HUMOR

I am not suggesting you be funny on paper if funny is not what you are. It does not work. Don't even try. It's like asking a hen to be a car.

I am also not suggesting that you yuk it up daily. Or wear a party hat when you write. Getting engaged in the process and reaping its rewards is not about going "ha ha."

I am talking about your approach and view. About balance. Perspective. And patience.

Now if you are not Type A, you're ahead of me here. You obviously have this stuff in the bag. But if you are—or have Type A tendencies—you should try to learn to chill.

Writing is work. Very hard work. It's demanding. And very intense. Ironically, you need to lighten up. Not only when you are away from your desk, but about what you are saying and how.

Without this balance, you may be unsufferable and suffocating. Both to your loved ones and to yourself. You will become The Unbearable Heaviness of Being.

Take writing seriously, but enjoy the ride. Step back. Give yourself a break. A break from the intensity of your labor. And from your more serious side.

Accept that your writing won't always be good. And your words won't all be pearls. And facing the blank page can be maddening and rough. As is facing form rejections.

The writing road is rocky. Patience and perspective are keys. Don't beat up on yourself. Or panic. Or call yourself a failure or fraud when it is not a happening day.

A writer's struggles are not like gym class from which a doctor friend of your family can write you a phony excuse. You will have them, so endure them. Struggling is part of the deal.

Don't get uptight when your words come out clunky.

Or when they aren't coming out at all.

Don't fall apart when the editor loses your manuscript.

Or when, without a word of explanation, she writes, "Sorry no."

Stand back. See the picture through the long lens. Be serious, not *just* serious though. You need a sense of humor. Some distance. A philosophical point of view.

You have delete buttons. Erasers. Correction fluid.

And better yet: tomorrow.

A DESIRE TO LEARN

Remember H.E.M. from an earlier section who took her toys and split? She had no interest in revising her work. She had no desire to learn.

No one gets anywhere with writing—with anything—with such a Bye, Bye Birdie and so long.

Decent writers can and do go far if they are also very good students. They are willing to learn. And to revise and revise. That's the only way to get better.

My student Mary wrote and revised a novel in my class, which was published to critical acclaim. When she first came to me, she had something there, but it came out sounding clunky. She soaked up our comments. She welcomed the criticism and went home each week to make changes. She took out sections, tightened others, eliminated characters that didn't work, beefed up others who needed more flesh. The published novel is nothing like what she initially brought to class. It's a beautiful, compelling book that works from start to finish.

Another student whom I will call Norman would rather publish than learn. He writes decent essays. They could be better, but he is not open to the process.

Instead of taking in the class's suggestions for revisions, he criticizes our criticism.

Defensiveness keeps one stuck.

You must push past your limits to keep growing.

A WILLINGNESS TO SHARE

To my mind, all good writing is self-revelatory. Which means letting others see your insides. This takes honesty, sincerity and courage. It means showing who you are.

If this goes against what you were told by your English teachers or parents or other authoritative adults, it's probably because they weren't such great campers at Tamakwa.

Or didn't know what to pack.

Mute the voices of all critics and adults who insist you keep on the lid. You can't be a good girl or dutiful son if you are going to write your truths.

When someone or something impedes your process, take a look at what's going on. You are writing for yourself now, not for anyone's approval.

Don't let fear stand in your way.

If you are not willing to share what is inside you, you would be better off selling lawn furniture or becoming a periodontist.

Advice

Think about the relationships, pursuits and experiences to which you brought or forgot the three items from Lou's list.

Think about their significance in your writing. In all your endeavors.

The keys are usually the same: patience, openness and perseverance.

CHAPTER TWELVE

Word Pictures

Open.

—The Dentist

$\mathcal{T}$here are essentially two ways to shape your experiences into pieces: through statements and word pictures. Statements are for telling, explaining, ruminating, offering your point of view and conveying truths directly. Word pictures are to *show*.

You can use both as beginnings and throughout your work. Weave them together as you structure your piece.

In this section, we are going to focus on word pictures as leads and how you can write your own.

A word picture is a scene. A scene that evokes a mood. You can create that mood by going directly back into the experience or incident you wish to write about.

How?

By putting yourself at the center of the scene and dramatizing what you went through. To do that, you must fully call up and connect to the feelings you had about the incident or experience. You need to relive them as you write.

Going right to the heart of the scene is one of the best ways to make readers care about what you are going to say. A good opening word picture invites them into your world. It hints at or promises what the piece or book is about.

Author Mary Karr opens *The Liar's Club*, her deeply felt bestselling memoir, with the following word picture:

> My sharpest memory is of a single instant surrounded by dark. I was seven, and our family doctor knelt before me where I sat on a mattress on the bare floor. He wore a yellow golf shirt unbuttoned so that sprouts of hair showed in a V shape on his chest. I had never seen him in anything but a white starched shirt and gray tie. The change unnerved me. He was pulling at the hem of my favorite nightgown—a pattern of Texas bluebonnets bunched into nosegays tied with ribbons against a field of nappy white cotton. I had tucked my knees under it to make a tent. He could easily have yanked the thing over my head with one motion, but something made him gentle. "Show me the marks," he said. "Come on, now. I won't hurt you."

Karr then goes on to describe the doctor's face quite vividly including his "mustache that looked like a caterpillar," has him talk to her some more, describes how he spoke "in that begging voice he used when he had a long needle behind his back" then reveals what she was feeling about being asked to hike up her nightgown in this dark bedroom she shared with her sister while strangers were "milling around in the living room."

A chilling picture of her dark, scary world. It's arresting. Haunting. Ambiguous. The reader isn't sure exactly what this is all about. Has the author been abused? Is that what the doctor wants to know? Or is he coming on to her? The reader wants these mysteries unraveled, so she reads on.

All I know is I am there. Really there. Dying to find out if he is trying to save or molest her. That opening scene is utterly compelling. Karr grabs readers by the neck.

What does she do to achieve this?

She puts herself right in the center or heart of the scene. There she is—right away in the first two opening sentences—a seven-year-old child surrounded by dark on a mattress on a bare floor with the family doctor kneeling before her.

We, as readers, are locked in that space with her. She puts herself and us right there. It's gripping. And vivid. And becomes even more vivid and textured with the specific details she gives of their clothes. The doctor didn't just wear a shirt. He wore "a yellow golf shirt unbuttoned so that sprouts of hair showed in a V shape on his chest." And Karr didn't just wear a nightgown. It had "a pattern of Texas bluebonnets bunched into nosegays tied with ribbons against a field of nappy white cotton."

She makes us use our senses. We not only get a picture of what the doctor and she were wearing, but then a description of his face and mustache.

Karr then goes even further. She has us hear the doctor's voice, through both the words he uses when he asks Karr to show him the marks, and with the actual sound of his voice too: She describes it as a "begging voice" comparing it to how it sounds when he is holding a long needle behind his back.

Do his words and voice sound sexual? Or paternal? We're still not really sure. But Karr's details give readers a compelling picture. They bring us into her world, feeling what she felt as a child. The utter loneliness and fear.

Another technique Karr uses to even further evoke our response as readers is to show both hers and the doctor's actions: He *pulled* at the hem of her nightgown; she *tucked* her knees under it to make a tent. That's action. Nothing's static. It's happening. And alive.

WORD PICTURES AS LEADS

In many of my personal essays, I use word pictures as leads. Here is how I began "One Sister's Song" that was published in *Parents* magazine:

> A scene from my childhood stands out vividly in my mind. It occurred more than 30 years ago. My older sister, Susan, and I were sitting in our parents' 1956 gray Buick in the parking lot of Mastman's Delicatessen where our mother was shopping. Usually I'd go in too because the woman at Mastman's bakery counter would give me a sample while waiting on my mother. Yet when Susan said that she'd stay in the car, I decided that I'd stay too. Time alone with my big sister meant more to me than Mastman's cookies.
>
> Even though we were not close as children, I truly believed that would change when we grew up. I even had a fantasy, a wonderful long-time fantasy—that we would own a dress shop or a candy store together. All day we'd wait on customers and discuss our merchandise. Then, at night, after closing our shop and going home to our families, we'd be on the phone talking over business and gossiping.
>
> As adults we'd be just like Lucy and Ethel or my father's two sisters, who were constantly on the phone or in each other's kitchen. I once shared my dress shop-candy store dream with Susan and although she was not enraptured by the idea, I was sure that one day she'd see the beauty of it and come around.
>
> "Let's sing our song," I now say in the car.
>
> With Susan's help, I had just made up the words and melody of a song and was feeling very heady about it. It went like this:
>
> "We are the sisters. The Davidoff sisters. We'll never

leave each other as long as we can stand it. My name is Susan (her solo). And my name is Nancy (my solo). We'll never leave each other as long as we can stand it."

Susan agrees to sing it with me one time. As soon as we begin, she bursts out laughing, then so do I. I'm in heaven. No rich chocolate cupcake could have filled me up as much.

"Let's do it again," I say.

Susan is looking out the window. She shakes her head.

"What about when Mom comes back? Will you do it for her?"

"No," she says emphatically.

"OK," I say, smiling an enormous smile. "We'll wait until we have the store and sing it for our customers."

She is avoiding my glance. "Nancy, please," she snaps.

My smile suddenly drops. Something inside me clicks. At that moment, I know in my gut that the chances of my ever owning a store with Susan are about the same as our flying to Never Never Land with Peter Pan and Tink.

With this opening picture, I went right into a childhood incident that was emotionally charged for me. It had been haunting me my whole life. That experience in the backseat of the car that day was as vivid for me when I wrote about it in 1992 as it was when I was eight. I could still see our '56 gray Buick. And feel the giddiness I felt back then when my mother pulled into the parking lot, got out of the car and went into Mastman's, giving me a chance to be alone with my sister to giggle and play and connect. The experience was so intense for me, it was easy to share the details.

I further evoke the mood through our actions, reactions and dialogue. My longing for closeness and my sister's wanting me to bug off come through with my staying in the car, fantasizing about our future with the dress or candy store, making up a song, singing it, getting giggly when my sister sings it with me, then showing my smile disappear and my mood suddenly change when she pushes me away with her emphatic "no" and then again with her "Nancy, please."

I am a person who hears voices. From the past. In the present. When I'm alone. I love writing dialogue. It is among my favorite things to write.

And also to read. Both with fiction and with nonfiction, I sometimes skip ahead to dialogue. It makes what is happening more immediate to me. It brings me to the center. People's words and voices invariably pull me in.

So if you are anything like me or the writers I know, you will probably have a penchant for writing what you prefer to read.

The next word picture is my beginning of "The Grandfather Connection," another *Parents* piece:

> My father and my daughter, Emily, thirteen, are doing the breaststroke side by side in the pool at my parents' condominium. About every half length, one looks over at the other, making sure neither has gotten ahead or behind. When they finish, they come over to where I'm sitting, grab their towels and dry off.
>
> "Papa did eight lengths today, Ma," Emily tells me exuberantly. "Isn't that just great?"
>
> I nod to her and to my father—my short, twinkly-eyed father—who is beaming at his only granddaughter. Yes, it's great. It has always been great between the two of them—both in and out of the water.
>
> Earlier, as they were getting into the pool, Emily had asked me whether I wanted to join them. I said no. Even though I am a swimmer, I usually say no when she asks. Doing laps has evolved into one of their activities. Three might be a crowd.

The two of them, now sitting in lounge chairs next to mine, look tired yet relaxed. I am envious of the pure, uncomplicated bond between them. Both of my grandfathers died long before I was born. I wish I had known them, since I see what my daughter gets from my father. *It's what I got from him, only more.*

That last sentence hints at what the rest of the piece is about: that a grandparent's love is simple, pure and unconditional, and devoid of parental expectations.

This opening scene has the three of us right there at the pool. I recreated a particular world. The condo poolside world. My daughter and father are fully engaged in action, swimming side by side in close proximity while I watch and ruminate from a distance. My reactions and response to their swimming together and to my daughter's words set the mood, show the loving bond between them and hopefully evoke the reader's response.

WORD PICTURES FOR TONE

At the beginning of this next *Parents* essay "Our Children, Ourselves" (November 1990), I use two word pictures with two sets of people to set the scene and tone:

> My daughter's friend Joanna stayed at our house one weekend when her parents were out of town. Friday evening, her mother called to see how everything was going. She and I chatted briefly before Joanna came to the phone.
>
> "If it's not too much trouble," she said, "would you make sure Joanna's sheet and blankets are tucked in tightly all around? She can't sleep when they're loose."
>
> Of course it was no trouble, yet at bedtime, as I was complying with this request, Joanna started to giggle.
>
> "My mother told you to do that, didn't she?" Joanna asked.

I nodded.

Joanna went on: "She can't sleep unless her bed is like an envelope, and she thinks I'm the same way. Isn't that funny?"

Not any funnier than going to a Chinese restaurant with my daughter, Emily, twelve, and our neighbors and hearing the following:

"Wanna share an order of egg rolls, or each get our own?" Emily asked David, our neighbors' twelve-year-old son.

Before he could reply, his father said, "David won't eat egg rolls. He doesn't like them."

Now, David definitely likes egg rolls. I know because just a few Sundays ago, he had an egg roll at our house—his father wasn't there—and guess what he said when he finished it: "Do we get seconds in egg roll?"

The rest of the piece is about how parents view their children as extensions of themselves. In the above two opening word pictures—with Joanna and the sheets, and David and the egg roll—I again use dialogue, actions and reactions.

I also share my point of view. I poke fun at these parents, who are sure they know their kids' minds. Yet, as I go on to show in the rest of the piece, I am one of them. So the humor becomes self-deprecating. I laugh at myself, too.

In "Our Children, Ourselves," I show readers my nudgy side. In "The Grandfather Connection," I am an observer who's out of the loop. And in the following *Parents* essay, "Waiting for Daddy," I show another aspect of myself as a mother: learning to do it alone.

This is the opening scene:

It's six o'clock on Friday—a warm, spring Friday evening. I just finished packing my five-year-old daughter Emily's overnight bag and she is now putting in her favorite stuffed animal and her new fruit-flavored lip balm. Her father is coming to pick her up for their weekend visit and she wants to wait outside where Jamie and Katy, her friends from the building, are trying Jamie's new bike.

I am right at the center of this scene on Friday night with my daughter. I show how we act and react. I packed her bag, now she is putting in favorite things while I watch her. I mention specific items. Then I share my daughter's desire to be outside with her friends.

When I sat down to write about this experience, I didn't know I'd eventually shape it into a piece. The feelings were there at the surface. I just let them come pouring out. They were available, and I readily accessed them. It beat keeping them bottled up.

PUTTING YOURSELF THERE

You have to visit and capture the scenes, experiences and incidents in your life that are emotionally charged.

That means putting yourself there again.

Intensely.

Feeling those emotions again.

And being fluid as they bubble up.

It's reliving it all on the paper.

It requires opening a vein.

The actress Irenie Worth was in a play with Alec Guinness and was awestruck by his genius. She was incredulous by the way he engaged audiences and wanted some of that magic. In a scene she was not in with him, she watched from the wings to see what it was he did.

You know what she discovered? He wasn't *doing* anything. *That* was his greatness. He was being. Fully being. Up there on that stage.

You have had incidents in your life that haunt you. You may

not be able to say why. No matter. If they are not right there and accessible to you, you can brainstorm or freewrite.

You have undoubtedly had experiences that left a great impact. A small loss. A struggle with yourself or a loved one. Or a far more shattering event.

Carla, my first student to publish suffered a serious blow. Her college boyfriend committed suicide. It was the subject of a moving essay she had published in *Cosmopolitan*. Here is how "My Lover Committed Suicide" begins:

> I opened my closet and cried. I had nothing to wear. I did have a beautiful black dress, but was it proper for me to wear black? After all, we had only lived together. Something navy or brown—or gray—would be better. I cried some more. I had nothing nice in any of those colors. I swore I heard a voice (I think it was my mother's) say, "Don't carry on so, Carla; it isn't as though you had any advance notice." But then another voice (unmistakably mine) said, "Oh yes, Carla, yes, you did."

She grabs her readers with this picture of herself standing in front of her closet deciding what to wear. In mentioning that she is choosing dresses from among several appropriate colors— black, navy, brown and gray—she not only brings us into her world and dilemma in a specific way, but creates a powerful and immediate bond with female readers.

You notice, too, that Carla never *tells* us what she is feeling. She *shows* us through her tears, her actions and the internal voices she hears. And that final line of the paragraph, with her mother's words and voice, complicates the situation further. Carla is not just grieving, but is beginning to feel the guilt. Guilt or at least some responsibility for her boyfriend's death. So yet another emotion is brought to fore and texturing the piece. Along with loss and pain and anguish, remorse is slowly creeping in.

Certain experiences in your life torment or haunt or amuse you. Or in some way make a huge dent. They impact in the moment. And again. And again.

Relive them on paper to see why.

Author and screenwriter/director Nora Ephron was visiting her mother in the hospital shortly before she died.

"Take notes," her mother, who had been a writer, told her.

Of course!

Literally or mentally, writers are always taking notes. We live our lives and observe them. We participate and stand back.

Playwright Neil Simon describes himself as a monster who observes the human being. Our behavior and that of the people to whom we relate or try to relate is our basic raw material.

When you sit down to write a personal experience piece, it is fine if you are not sure what you want to say. It is enough that an idea or experience is obsessing you. The point will come as you write. Occasionally the idea or point comes full blown. More often it comes as we write. Sometimes we don't get to it for several drafts.

To create vivid word pictures, write about the things you *really* care about. The experiences that play over and over in your heart and mind. If you feel passionately about your subject, it will come through on the page.

Advice

Close your eyes and picture an incident that has been obsessing you. List the details and images you recall. Write what was said. And what was not.

Jot down yours and others' actions and reactions. Think about why the effect was so profound.

The experiences that have touched or hurt or tickled you are the material from which Your Truths spring. Look at them. Pore over them. See what plays over in your heart and mind. There are reasons why some obsess us. They are the stuff about which we write.

Exercise

Write about the above childhood incident or another that is still very much alive for you today.

Create the scene. Put yourself right there. Show your actions and reactions and those of the other people who were there.

Let's hear you talk.

Use specific details that make the readers use their senses.

Make it as evocative and immediate as you can.

No one's wearing a stopwatch. Take time to dig and sort and probe and make notes.

CHAPTER THIRTEEN

Statements as Leads

Some women don't get it. It's not about lots of jewelry or color. "Take it off. Take it all off," I want to tell them. "Just wear the little black dress."

—*Judy, my fashion-designer friend*

Again, when you begin with a word picture, you set the scene, *show* the world you are creating and put yourself at its center. That means reliving the experience, calling up the feelings and getting it all down.

To do that, you must be willing to show who you are inside. And of course, you must really care.

Write from your heart, not from anywhere else. Otherwise, it won't ring true. If you are engaged, readers will be, too.

THE DIRECT APPROACH

If you do not start off with a word picture, then use a direct, straightforward lead. A sentence or two will often do. Sometimes you will need more. They should be compelling, honest, simple and fresh. And set the tone for the entire work.

Author Anna Quindlen does this quite effectively with her essays. She gets readers in the mood with a good loud bang.

Here is a lead of one of her pieces (from *Living Aloud*, Random House, 1988):

> I was a Paul girl. Still am, I suppose, at the core.

That is the beginning of an essay about the appeal of each of the Beatles, particularly Paul and John, how both Paul and she have changed since 1964.

A grabbing opener. For several reasons, too. It's simple, direct and revealing. Quindlen shares her point of view—as she regularly does—with an unusual phrase. Stating that she is "a Paul girl" is a whole lot fresher than merely saying that she favors Paul. "Paul girl" catches the reader's attention. We're curious enough to sit back and read on to find out what it means.

And since so many of us had "favorite Beatles"—the cool kids tended to go for Paul, the bohemians went for John—we want to know how Quindlen perceives them to see how we stack up.

My student Michele began her *Times* (December 10, 1995) essay, "Hunting for a New Therapist," with the following direct statements:

> I was shopping for a new shrink.
>
> The psychiatrist I had been seeing for almost two years was forty-five minutes and three subways from my office. Too many sessions were being spent analyzing the subway, and twice a week I was making a night out of a shrink appointment. I wanted therapy to be part of my life, not prevent me from having one.

After that lead, she takes us into the offices of the therapists she consults with word pictures *showing* through their interaction or lack of it how screwy they all are until she finds one who has a nodding acquaintance with reality and with whom she had an instant rapport.

Michele's lead is simple and funny. The word "shrink" sets

up a humorous tone. And her subject is a winner. She promises us a joyful romp. So many people see shrinks and don't tell.

STATE YOUR PURPOSE

When opening with a statement or a few, be simple, be clear, be honest. Say what the piece is about. Here is my opening paragraph of an essay, "Lifelong Friends" (*Parents*, March 1993):

> They became part of my life long ago: Inez in the first grade, Cindy in the seventh and Doreen on the first day of college. I remember what initially drew me to them and why I wanted them as friends.

Those two sentences are actually topic sentences. The *second* is precisely what the piece is about. The rest of the piece is comprised of scenes or word pictures of my first encounters with all three, capturing that certain something that made me click with each and how that something still exists today.

"Old Dad" (*New York Times*, April 28, 1996, p. 84—Lives), Roger Wilkins's essay about being an older father, also begins with direct statements:

> Recently, a friend of my grown daughter, Amy, was surprised to learn that she had a sister and asked:
> "What does she do?"
> "Fifth grade," Amy replied.
> Amy will be 37 this year, her brother, David, will be 32, and her sister, Elizabeth, will be 13.

Like Michele's, the author's tone is humorous. Amy's response when asked what her sister does surprises readers. We are not expecting "fifth grade."

As readers, we like to be surprised or tickled or amused. When a writer starts off by saying it funny or in a fresh or unusual way, he is promising a delightful, illuminating ride. We can take off our shoes, sit back and relax.

Chances are we're in the hands of a pro.

On the subject of pros, let's take a look at a master. None other than E.B. White. His essays are jewels. I know of none better. His touching "The Second Tree From the Corner" begins with this lead:

> I spent several days and nights in mid-September with an ailing pig and I feel driven to account for this stretch of time, more particularly since the pig died at last, and I lived, and things might easily have gone the other way and none left to do the accounting.

It is introspective, understated, funny, economical and simple. Perfect in every way. Great is great. I can say no more. Let us just recognize genius, be grateful White was among us and look at his work in awe.

BOOM! BOOM! BOOM!

When you write a straightforward lead, get to it right away. Hint at what you are writing about. Share your point of view. Set the mood or tone. Tell it like it is.

A friend wrote an essay she asked me to read. The beginning had blades of grass.

It also had squirrels. And trees with leaves falling. It was a cluttered mess.

There was no scene with her in it. Or statement saying what to expect.

"What is the essay about?" I asked.

She hemmed and hawed and sputtered, then said, "It's about how nurtured I feel at my mother's."

Yeah?

So why was my stomach growling? Because I was hungry to go into her world with either a word picture or a simple sentence or two.

I start twitching when people beat around the bush. In person and on the page. I love direct, simple statements and calling a spade a spade.

Like the way Joyce Wadler begins her book titled *My Breast*:

> I have a scar on my left breast, four inches long, which runs from the right side of my breast to just about the nipple. Nick, who I no longer see, once said, if anyone asked, I should say I was attacked by a jealous woman. The true story, which I prefer, is that a surgeon made the cut, following a line I had drawn for him the night before.

Or Anna Quindlen's being "a Paul girl."

Or Michele's "shopping for a new shrink."

Get in. Get in quickly. Boom! Boom! Boom! Boom! Boom!

Honest. Fresh. Straightforward.

Say it in your own special way.

The best in us—at least what I most love—is simplicity with heart.

Advice

Read *The Essays of E.B. White.*

Read *Charlotte's Web* and *Stuart Little*. And read *The Elements of Style*, by Strunk and White.

Read everything you can get your hands on by E.B. White.

Exercise

List three relationships between you and someone you would like to write about in some way. Take the one that is leaping out or hitting the hardest now.

Write a direct sentence about it. State what you wish to say.

Think of this sentence as a topic sentence, like the kind your English teachers told you to write. Make it as fresh and unusual and inviting and revealing as possible.

Does it make you giggle or cringe or leap?

Continue writing the piece.

Later go back and write about the other two. Or about others that are bubbling up.

CHAPTER FOURTEEN

Now What?

To find a form that accommodates the mess, that is the task of the artist now.

—*Samuel Beckett*

How do you keep readers in the tent after pulling them in with your lead?

By giving them an illuminating, engaging read with truths, sincerity and self-revelatory scenes.

That means staying in the tent yourself using one or more dramatic scenes.

In *The Liar's Club*, which we discussed in the previous chapter, author Mary Karr does just that. At the beginning she is there as a seven-year-old child, in her house in a small oil town in Texas. A strong image is already in the reader's mind. Then the picture becomes increasingly bleak and Karr's fears even more palpable in successive scenes in that house, in others, in bars and on trips with her crazy, alcoholic family. Each member is a fully fleshed-out person. Complicated. And pained.

Her descriptions are fresh and specific. Karr uses telling details to describe them physically. What makes them even more real to the reader is that she shows them fully in action, drinking, going crazy, hurting each other, abandoning the children and telling lies. Using her sharp powers of observation to give readers vivid, telling details, putting them into action and having them speak, Karr makes them so immediate and textured they practically leap off the page.

The reader is there with Karr in her gritty world. The atmosphere is highly charged. The images are powerful. The pain is deeply felt throughout.

Yet Karr also comes across as warm and humane. Despite her parents' and grandmothers' problems and the lack of stability she faced, she manages to see the humor in her situation. Lucky for her. And for us. From the outset, the reader likes her, identifies with her and cares.

In reliving her childhood, Karr profoundly feels the pain. The tense atmosphere in which she grew up, the troubled, lost adults who inhabited it, and the family dynamics that shaped her are depicted in powerful, immediate images. The reader is there feeling the anguish and fearing what will happen next.

While reading *The Liar's Club*, I was in that Texas oil town, forgetting my own surroundings. The writing is simple and sparce. And seamless. One does not notice the words. They are there to create a world and evoke the reader's response.

The author has the reader on edge throughout. And totally enthralled.

VIVID SCENES

So does my student Carla in her essay "My Lover Committed Suicide" (discussed in chapter twelve, "Word Pictures"). After *showing* us what she is going through before the funeral as she opens her closet door and contemplates what she will wear, she flashes back to another dramatic scene: one at college after her boyfriend's death:

Months after Richard died, I came across a book in the lounge of the campus chapel. At first I couldn't bring myself to hold it in my hands. I felt as if I had some dreadful disease I'd chosen to ignore, and suddenly this book, this pamphlet, would bring all my symptoms into focus—and I would find out I was dying. I eyed the cover for a few moments: a cover adorned with brilliant splashes of color and the words *After Suicide*. I sifted through all the facts and figures, appalled and comforted that there were enough cases to make a statistical study. And I read this: Most suicides occur on a Friday, before the weekend: or on a Sunday, before the work week commences.

Following that is another scene:

But this was a Wednesday. I had come home late from class. Richard had already eaten. I didn't cook for him that night. He played his guitar for a little while in the living room while I studied in the bedroom. At around ten-thirty, he put on his jacket and announced he was going for a ride on his motorcycle.

Carla then ruminates about their relationship, about who he was and what he meant to her, alternately using statements and other scenes with her and Richard *in action*, and *talking* until her final touching one.

You can use several word pictures or you can have just one.

In "The Grandfather Connection," which I previously discussed, I not only remain in the same scene throughout (at the pool of my parents' condominium) but also in the same position (sitting on a lounge chair watching and listening to my daughter and my father):

My father, opening his eyes now from a little snooze, asks us the time.

Emily immediately answers, "Time for the story

about how you practiced for Cousin Herb."

No, not again, I groan to myself. I have heard this story too many times when I was growing up, and in recent years with Emily. But as I glance over at my father—who is sitting up, fully awake and raring to go—and then at my daughter, who is eagerly waiting—I think "Ah yes, again."

When my father was growing up, he lived next door to his Cousin Herb. The two boys took violin lessons together, only Herb never quite caught on. Afraid to tell his mother, Herb talked my father into practicing for him. Every evening, my dad would climb out through his bedroom window and sneak into Herb's room, where he would practice their lesson—for a quarter.

"Didn't your parents know?" Emily asks.

"For a dime, I had my brother cover for me," he tells her.

"What about Herb's parents?" she responds.

"He had a brother too."

"Didn't you feel funny taking Herb's quarters?"

"Never."

Unlike Carla and Mary Karr, I do not give readers a sense of the place and people through details and description. It is among the many reasons why I am in awe of Karr. She creates a sense of immediacy, in part, by using specific details. If I had to describe the grass beneath my feet, I would struggle to make the reader see and feel it.

I dramatize more through dialogue. In the above scene, I have my father and daughter talk. Here and in many of my pieces, dialogue is one of the techniques I use to depict a relationship, create a sense of immediacy, and bring the reader into my world. When my father tells stories about himself, he is charged up. And has so much to give.

My daughter gets a kick out of hearing him. I am sitting a little apart from them watching and feeling quite pleased. She is learning that it is OK—more than OK—to bend the rules now and then as long as no one gets hurt. It keeps the spirit alive. Better she learns from my father that it's fine to have secrets. Things a mother shouldn't know.

I continue to dramatize their relationship through their actions and words—Emily sees some ducks in a little pond and goes to watch them. My father follows her. And they stay close together. Side by side. Looking into the water. I don't get up from the lounge chair. I remain the observer. The outsider who does not join in.

Then to further dramatize their bond, I sit there with my memories of how my father has acted and reacted in the past.

> I think now of the thousands of times Emily has said, "I love you" to my father at the end of their phone conversations and at bedtime when we visit. He melts when he hears these words, just as he did when she visited him in the hospital over a year ago after he'd had surgery. He was surly to my mother when she tried to feed him. He behaved a little better for me, but when he saw Emily, his mood immediately changed. His entire face lit up.

In the above, my father's different response towards my mother, then me and then my daughter, sums up and again dramatizes the relationship.

MIXING PICTURES WITH STATEMENTS

When you begin your work with a declarative sentence, you can then give one or more word pictures, alternating them with direct statements using the same structure as you would if you had opened with a scene.

My student Allan Ishac begins "A Son's Vigil" with a moving

essay about having a father who is sixty-one years older than he with the following hard-hitting statement:

> I was 7 years old when I first realized that most people my father's age were dead.

What immediately follows is this word picture:

> There was a newspaper left open to the obituary page on our kitchen table, and as my eyes scanned the bold print listing names and ages, the linoleum under my feet grew soft and unsteady. If there is a moment in a child's life when the world turns frightening, my secret fears began that day.

Notice how he reveals what he felt in the context of this scene. He follows this with more statements:

> My father was 61 when I was born and well into old age by the time I learned that death was final, that it happened to every living thing and, generally, to old things first. That made my father dangerously ripe for the reaper, and it wrapped my own early life in a shroud.

Then he has another scene, more statements and keeps on alternating the two until a final arresting scene in which he comes to his truth about the complexity of their bond.

The above examples show you ways to shape your pieces through dramatic scenes. Sometimes you can stay in one. Other times you can use several. Your statements and ruminations can come between the scenes. Or in them.

Whatever you are writing, think "scenic."

LAST WORDS

Now what about the ending?

The ending is, as I see it, your summation. Your truth. The point you are driving home.

One technique I regularly and unwittingly use is to have dialogue right before the end. *Those last words* spoken by me or by someone else usually capture the essence of the piece, the "aha" at which I arrive.

My universal truth in "The Grandfather Connection" is that the love between a grandparent and child is unconditional and among the purest there is. On that note, I end with the following:

> Emily's expression today when she reported that my father had swum eight lengths was not much different.
>
> "Isn't that just great?" she had said.
>
> It's more than just great. The two of them stand close together now, watching the ducks come back up to the shore. . . . It's simple and special and pure. It's the buddy system at its best.

In the above, I have Emily talking. Then I close with what I see and feel. My "aha" about their connection. A connection I don't quite have.

Here is my final scene of "Lifelong Friends," the piece about my relationship with my three longtime girlfriends. It is at our high school reunion, using Cindy's voice and mine:

> The sharp crowd saved a seat—one—for her at their table. She didn't take it. She took a seat next to me.
>
> "You didn't have to do that," I said.
>
> "I know," she replied, "but they were then, and you are always."
>
> "I'm touched."
>
> "Very," she said. "That's why I'm here."

Then in my last paragraph, I return to my feelings and truth:

> Bless her! Bless Inez and Doreen, too. They're not family, but at times they've been more. I rarely see them, but their presence in my life still matters. And always will.

The ending, I believe, should in some way go back to you and your take. Most of the essays with which I am familiar end similarly to the above, with the author commenting on or summing up what someone thought or said right before.

Nora Ephron ends her "A Few Words About Breasts," a piece about how she felt growing up flat-chested, with her reaction to her voluptuous friends giving her a litany of their misfortunes:

> I have thought about their remarks, tried to put myself
> in their place, considered their point of view. I think they
> are full of shit.

You can also end with your own snippet of dialogue—spoken or imagined.

Here's Anna Quindlen's ending from a piece on her marriage. "Husbands and Boyfriends" is about how the man she fell in love with was not real husband material. More Rhett Butler than Ashley Wilkes. She goes into the reasons why it's all wrong. Yet what she comes to at the end is that if he were to scandalize a Confederate ball, as Rhett did, by bidding $150 in gold to dance with her, would she consider it? She writes:

> I know what I would say without a moment's hesita-
> tion. "Oh yes, I will."

Whether the last sentence or few is your own imagined or real dialogue or your take on someone else's in the form of a statement, it should not only reveal something to the readers about who you are and what you think and feel, but who they are as well.

You want to touch or tickle the reader or hit her over the head with a feeling, a thought or an insight that will linger.

It can make her pause. Or smile. Or nod.

Here's my ending of "One Sister's Song":

> . . . childhood fantasies don't die so easily. Recently,
> after reading an article I had written, Susan offered her
> praise.

"It's great that you've carved out such a nice career," she said.

"I had no choice," I told her. "You didn't want to open up the dress shop."

She laughed. Then I laughed too. Only a part of me wasn't kidding.

That conversation and final sentence crystallize my truth. About my relationship with my sister.

About a whole lot more.

Advice

Read the essay collections of Anna Quindlen, Nora Ephron and whomever else you admire to see how they build their pieces and what they do at the end.

CHAPTER FIFTEEN

Three Components of a Personal Experience Piece

Human life itself may be almost pure chaos, but the work of the artist . . . is to take these handfuls of confusion and disparate things . . . and put them together in a frame to give them some kind of shape and meaning.

—Katherine Ann Porter

The scenes, statements and dialogue provide the framework for what you are saying.

And what *are* you saying, anyway? *You must say something.*

You cannot just let off steam.

And you can't just whine or kvetch.

No one is in the market for your complaints except for psychotherapists. And Lord knows what they are *really* thinking as they watch that clock and nod.

To touch the hearts and minds of your readers and make your personal experiences come alive, your work should have three components.

A POINT OF VIEW

This is your unique or special way of viewing your experience. It is your take. Your vantage point. *Your you.* It is not the world according to your mother, your spouse, John Irving or Garp. It is the world the way you see it. The world according to you.

When Anna Quindlen writes, "I was a Paul girl. Still am, I suppose, at the core," she tells readers who her favorite Beatle was. In the rest of the piece, she shares why. In the above lead, she reveals something about who she was as a teenager. She gives us her point of view.

In "A Son's Vigil," a published essay we discussed in a previous chapter, author Allan Ishac writes about what he went through having a father who was sixty-one years older than he. His vantage point or way of seeing the world was, of course, through the eyes of a son.

In "Old Dad," a *Times* essay also discussed in an earlier section, the author writes about having two grown children and becoming a father for the third time decades later. He sees the world now through the eyes of an older father. That is his point of view.

In the beginning of "My Lover Committed Suicide," we see the author on the day of the funeral opening herself up as she opens her closet door trying to decide what she should wear. She draws her readers into her world, and as she flashes back to her first encounter with her boyfriend and traces the relationship, we are right there beside her. In capturing her experience, she got under her skin, showing us how the experience affected her, sharing her point of view.

In "The Grandfather Connection," I see the special bond between my child and my dad from the point of view of a mother watching them swim together from my lounge chair. I am an outside observer. Not sharing or a part of their thing. My point of view in "One Sister's Song" is of an adoring eight-year-old girl who wanted to play with my big sister every waking moment and be the best of friends.

Getting under your skin is crucial. You can't simply rehash events. You must take a look at the experience and its impact. You must be willing to share how you feel.

You can get your point of view across in a variety of ways: in conversations, in dramatic scenes, through straightforward statements. You can be subtle or very direct.

There should be, at the very least, a hint of it at the beginning of your work so readers know what to expect. Reading for pleasure is not guesswork. We have far too much of that.

And if you are blessed with a sense of humor, *that* is your point of view. E.B. White, quoted in an earlier chapter, lets readers know in his opening paragraph that he lived, the pig didn't and had it been the other way around, there would be no one to "do the accounting."

Author Anne Lamott's book *Operating Instructions* is a humorous account of her first year of motherhood. She sets the tone right away. Here is part of her opening paragraph:

> I woke up with a start at 4:00 one morning and realized that I was very, very pregnant. What tipped me off was that, lying on my side and needing to turn over, I found myself unable to move. My first thought was that I had had a stroke.

Whether you get your point of view across directly or between the lines, it must in some way come through. You don't have to know what it is when your idea comes to you or even when you start to write your piece. At some point, though, you do.

ARRIVAL AT SOME BASIC TRUTH

As a result of the experience, something should become clear to you. You should reach a new level of understanding that you convey to your readers.

In *Operating Instructions*, Anne Lamott discovers that parenting, like life, is a mixed bag. There is joy as well as grief and just when we are ready to tear our hair out, the light shines on us again.

In more than one way and more than one time, particularly when she is at her wit's end, she realizes no one is perfect. Or has the answers. We are all just muddling through. The best we can do is love and forgive ourselves.

> . . . it helps beyond words to take yourself through
> the day as you would your most beloved mental-patient
> relative, with great humor and lots of small treats.

One morning at dawn when she is nursing her son, she decides that she is . . .

> probably just as good a mother as the next repressed,
> obsessive-compulsive paranoiac.
> I think we're all pretty crazy on this bus. I'm not sure
> I know anyone who's got all the dots on his or her dice.

You must, as shown in the above, come to some "aha" from the experience you are writing about.

A universal truth.

I have an acquaintance—I will call him Dave—who asked me to read his work. The subject of his essays is his divorce and since I have mined my own for publication and teach "Writing From Personal Experience," he thought I could show him The Way.

I wanted to like Dave's work. I didn't. It contained mundane details about lawyers' visits, his ex's move to Florida and his children's refusal to talk to him. He rehashed his experiences without ever saying what they meant to him or what he truly felt.

He catalogued events without ever looking at them or getting beneath the surface.

You can't just write: "I consulted a bunch of lawyers. My ex is in another state. My kids don't get on the phone."

What about that?

You have to go somewhere with the information or events you are putting on paper. You have to dig and probe and share with readers what the information means to you.

Dave did not do that with his divorce material. He didn't put himself at the center of this experience. He didn't show who he was or open himself up to his reader.

Good writing has revelations. Readers want truths about their own lives.

My student Carla, through her anguish over her boyfriend's suicide, came to realize that no matter how much she loved him, she could not have prevented his death, thus arriving at the truth that each of us is responsible for his own life.

In "Hunting for a New Therapist," also discussed earlier, my student Michele trails readers through her consultations with therapists, each nuttier than the one before, arriving at the basic truth that it's hard to make real connections, but when we do, we should grab them. Being understood is coming home.

You don't have to know what truth you are going to arrive at when you set out to write a piece anymore than you needed to know your point of view. It, too, can take time unraveling. My truths often arrive after a draft or two. They are rarely full blown in the beginning.

EMOTIONAL INVOLVEMENT

Emotional involvement means showing up fully and putting your heart into what you say.

Author and columnist Russell Baker does so movingly in his two memoirs: *Growing Up* and *Good Times*. Here is the beginning of the former:

At the age of eighty my mother had her last bad fall, and after that her mind wandered free through time. Some days she went to weddings and funerals that had taken place half a century earlier. On others she presided over family dinners cooked on Sunday afternoons for children who were now gray with age. Through all this she lay in bed but moved across time, traveling among the dead decades with a speed and ease beyond the gift of physical science.

"Where's Russell?" she asked one day when I came to visit at the nursing home.

"I'm Russell," I said.

She gazed at the improbably overgrown figure out of an inconceivable future and promptly dismissed it.

"Russell's only this big," she said, holding her hand, palm down, two feet from the floor . . .

Early one morning she phoned me in New York. "Are you coming to my funeral today?" she asked.

It was an awkward question with which to be awakened. "What are you talking about, for God's sake?" was the best reply I could manage.

"I'm being buried today," she declared briskly, as though announcing an important social event.

"I'll phone you back," I said and hung up, and when I did phone back she was all right, although she wasn't all right, of course, and we all knew she wasn't.

What does Baker do in the above to become so emotionally involved and in turn involve readers?

In his first paragraph, he puts a powerful image in the reader's mind. He captures his mother's condition simply, elegantly and in a very straightforward but understated way. There is heart, but no mush. The images he uses and the way he turns a phrase are beautiful and fresh. He brings the reader right into the world with a clear, unsentimental picture of his mother "presiding over family dinners" and attending weddings and funerals from her past while lying in her nursing home bed.

Those images are evocative. Strong. Unusual. Baker takes us right to her bedside with him. He brings the reader into that nursing home room, giving us a close-up of the action. It's as if we are witnessing it firsthand.

The tone is perfect. There's a lovable voice. Baker sees it—as he sees everything—with the humorist's eye.

Then right after the opening paragraph there is dialogue. This further enhances the sense of immediacy. It is no ordinary dialogue either. His mother asks him, "Where's Russell?"

Pretty funny. Pretty sad.

A strong reaction is evoked in the reader by those two simple words.

Baker doesn't call his mother "confused" or label her anything else. His startling initial images coupled with her now asking "Where's Russell?" says it all.

The rest of this opening section is in dialogue that continues to enhance the sense of immediacy. The conversation with his mother becomes even more hilarious, yet right under the surface of the hilarity is excruciating sadness and pain.

There is so much going on here and so many emotions deeply felt with just a few short, simple phrases. Baker's humor, humanity and warmth are there in the dialogue and in the images he plants in the reader's minds. The atmosphere is charged. The reader is tickled and touched. Baker's genius is there in spades.

Stan Getz said he never played a note he didn't mean. It's the same with Baker's words.

He felt what happened in that nursing home room.

Mean what you write and write what you mean. Otherwise it won't ring true.

Pat Conroy claims that what moves him to write and to feel is the power of his mother's voice. She told him, "Never write anything you cannot feel, never write anything without emotion, never write anything without passion."

Exactly.

Advice

Read Baker and Conroy.

More Advice

When you write about your experience, feel what you felt back then. There must be a universality in the emotions you dramatize, not necessarily in the experience.

Exercise

Think about an experience (e.g., a death, an illness, a birth, an accomplishment, a failure, a move, a celebration, a moment) that got under your skin and comes back to haunt you today.

Is there a picture or two in your mind?

Think about it. Visualize it. Some details must still be quite vivid and sharp. What are they? Write them down.

Think, too, about what was said. The things you reacted to strongly. That made you feel happy. Angry. Hurt. Rejected. Loved. Alone.

That made you feel something.

Write down the snippets of dialogue you can recall. Or the gist of what was said.

Remember, of course, how you felt. Write down

some of the adjectives. Then remember your actions and reactions and those of the others in the situation. Write down those that conveyed your feelings. The ones you just described with adjectives.

Now delete those adjectives.

Don't use them in your writing to describe how you feel. Use the behavior, the action, the dialogue and telling details.

If you were lonely, show physically and/or emotionally how you isolated yourself.

If you were angry, how did you react?

If you were embarrassed, did you hide it and act cool, start stuttering, talk incessantly so no one would notice, or turn red?

Your descriptions, actions and dialogue will plant images in the reader's mind and evoke a response.

CHAPTER SIXTEEN

How to Put the Components to Work

In deep silence we return to the ultimate case, pure Being.
There you come face-to-face with the womb of creation, the
source of all that was, is, will be, which is simply yourself.
　　　—Deepak Chopra

People read for several reasons: to learn, to grow and to be entertained. Readers are always hungry for something to chew on. Bring your goodies to the table. Make your writing sing.

If you put yourself at the heart of the experience, view it in your own special way and arrive at a wonderful "aha," you will educate and touch readers. And if you have a sense of the ridiculous, twinkling eyes or a twisted mind, you might just tickle them too.

To go about doing that when shaping your life into prose:

CARE ABOUT WHAT YOU WRITE ABOUT

Pick an experience you care about deeply. It can be an obsession, a relationship or a struggle in your life that you feel compelled to examine and understand.

If you write what you think you "should" write and not what is in your gut, you would be better off doing corporate reports or ghosting thank-you notes for friends.

Write about your struggles. Your unfinished business. Your dilemmas. And your questions. Having answers at the outset is bad news for good writing. If you have an "attitude" or are a "know-it-all," you won't be likable or even tolerable as you put yourself on the page.

Gilda Radner, Joyce Wadler and Betty Jane Rollin all wrote wonderful books about their battles with cancer. William Styron and Art Buchwald wrote books about their struggles with depression. Elizabeth Swados gave a clear, unsentimental picture of her family with its deaths, dependencies and destruction in her moving book, *The Four of Us*. So did Geoffrey Douglas in *Class: The Wreckage of an American Family*.

Suicide figured heavily into Swados's book. It was also the subject of my student Carla's first published piece and Calvin Trillin's memoir, *Remembering Denny*.

You need not have been to hell and back to turn your life into prose. Or invent ways in which you might suffer. Relationships, moments, small experiences and telling battles are material. As long as you have what to say.

My student Michele, who sold an essay on shrink shopping (mentioned in chapter thirteen), wrote another about her two dogs. She wanted her golden retrievers, Willi and Dune, to have unleashed quality time at the neighborhood dog run. But what a time she had getting them in. She wrote a delightful personal essay about what the admittance people put her and the two dogs through. She sold it to the *Times*. It was published on the Op-Ed page (May 11, 1996) and titled "They Don't Take Just Any Mutt."

Write about things that niggle at you. Things you struggle to sort out for yourself. Things that haunt, puzzle, enrage or tickle you. Things about which you obsess.

My child has been one of my Bigtime topics. She is at the center of my life. I have covered her at every age and from every angle from her crib days through her "Chill Ma" teens.

When she was a tiny peanut of a person and not yet sleeping through the night, she inspired my first piece, "A New Mother's Confessions of Ambivalence" (*Times*, Op-Ed, April 1977). It actually began as random notes I was writing in my journal. I was so overwhelmed by the profoundly conflicting feelings—the intense love I felt for her on the one hand and the awesome responsibility of raising her on the other—that I stayed up after the two A.M. feedings to get my feelings down. These feelings continued to pour out of me. I played with them, cutting and adding and switching things around, and eventually a piece evolved.

I mined our relationship, complexities, struggles and joys in dozens of essays as she grew. I wrote about a memorable Valentine's Day, my wishes for her and many about my divorce. As she got older, I wrote about her camp days, a bathing suit shopping excursion and what she and I learned from her friends. And underneath everything I say on these subjects is all I have learned as a mom.

Motherhood provides a wellspring of material for writers. Anne Lamott's book *Operating Instructions* which we discussed earlier, is about what she experienced as a single mother during her son's first year of life. Judith Viorst and Anna Quindlen have written extensively about their experiences with their children. Both writers are mothers of three.

Writers live their lives and look at them. We are "two-headed monsters" as Neil Simon says. We have experiences and relationships, then take two steps back to sort them out. To ponder. To scratch our heads.

"How do you pick what you write about?" a friend asked.

I write about my questions, and the relationships and incidents in my life that obsess me. The things that are inside me deeply.

That play over in my heart and mind.

"I don't pick my subjects," I told her. "I think that they pick me."

You should have the same feelings when you turn your experiences into words. If you don't care about your subject, it simply won't ring true.

And if you don't care, why should anyone else?

Exercise

List three relationships in your life that are or have been close. If you have been afraid to think or write about them, all the more reason to do so now.

Write a few sentences about each.

Continue with the one evoking the strongest reactions and most churning you up inside.

DON'T MAKE PUBLICATION YOUR PRIMARY GOAL

Although you may eventually hope to see your work in print, you shouldn't make publication your primary goal. Your initial satisfaction should come from writing and the discoveries you make in the process.

If you are not writing because you want to write, you should do something else. Writing is hard work. Really hard work. There are easier ways to be miserable.

In my twenties, I wrote—in addition to the personal pieces that were always most dear to my heart—profiles, short features and interviews for magazines and newspapers. It required stringing words together, which I found challenging and fun. I had a good time doing that. It was heady. It was cool.

Then I became pregnant. Suddenly I was talking to myself more than I ever had before.

Initially, my turning inward totally freaked me out. Did becoming a mother mean focusing exclusively on us? Would I forget the outside world? What worried me more than anything else was that I would become a crashing bore.

My journal entries clearly reflected this shift, the change in my focus and concerns. They were less about me in the world and more about what I'd be like as a mom. I was about to become responsible for a whole new other life. I looked outward less and less. I was beginning virtually all my entries with three words: "Hello in there."

I was writing, I realized, not just to my unborn child, but to this brand new, scared little me. I was uncovering more of myself. I was giving birth to two.

When I began jotting down my feelings about motherhood in my journal, I had no idea I would eventually shape them into a piece and then send it out to the *Times*. I was bursting with a whole new set of emotions I felt compelled to look at and understand.

My giving birth profoundly affected my writing. Better things began to emerge. About becoming a mother. About becoming more myself. About everything.

Once I stopped doing profiles, reviews and "out there" pieces for publication, writing became more fulfilling.

Many of my students write because they want to write. They keep at it and revise and improve. Often they publish, because they keep at it and get better. And better. And better.

I have other students who are in a hurry for bylines and agents. More often than not, they get neither. They are too busy marketing and talking about selling to sit down and write and grow.

It is really quite simple and it is how much in life happens. It is akin to falling in love. We get what we want when we let it happen and move out of our own way.

If getting published is your driving force, there is a good chance it will elude you. When you write first and foremost for yourself, not an audience or fame, you become a better writer. Then the audience finds you.

Important things take a long time to develop. That's what my mother used to say. I'm not sure I fully got her drift until I made the commitment to write.

Writing well takes practice. You get better the more you write. People in professions and in the other arts serve long apprenticeships. Writers are not excused.

Another thing about publication is that it is really no great shakes. Admittedly, it is a hoot to see one's name on a book cover on in a newspaper or magazine. It is a validation of our labor. A nod to what we do. It is them out there putting us on the map, legitimizing our solitude.

Everyone is a little nicer to us on publication day. For a few days, the relatives call. When the building handyman comes up to fix the toilet, he might say, "So that's why you're home all day."

But the boost to the ego is short-lived. The accolades quickly die down. Far more sustaining and nourishing is regularly expressing what is within.

Advice

Think about the reasons you really want to write.

Is it because you like the process or because you want the relatives to call?

Exercise

Jot down your reasons for writing. You don't have to show them to anyone.

DON'T WRITE JUST TO VENT

I qualified the above with the word "just." Otherwise, you may start venting.

In a Bigtime Way.

At me.

After all, I have been hounding you on every page in every way to be courageous, authentic and real. So am I telling you now to stifle yourself? To put a lid on all that's not sweet?

No.

And yes! If whining is all you're about.

We have all had lives that are less than idyllic. Let us count the blows: illnesses, rejection, abuse, death and divorce. And those less wrenching ones, too: being the butt of inhumane or shabby treatment from a person or from the system are a few.

Admittedly writers have axes to grind. There is "stuff" we did not get. Our struggles with ourselves and with our worlds is our material. It is one of the reasons we write. The passion and energy to put it down comes from what is missing or out of whack.

The best thing a writer can have, according to Pat Conroy, is an unhappy childhood.

Yep!

But . . .

Simply having pain, or something to kvetch about, or frustrations or anger to vent is *not* a reason to write. It is a reason to consult a therapist, tie up the phone wires with a best friend, do affirmations, write letters to editors, become an activist or join a consciousness-raising group.

Having anger to vent *is* a reason to write *if* it is one—only one—of the feelings that emerges. And if you are willing to look at it, examine it and see the other, deeper feelings lying underneath.

Dave, from an earlier chapter who had written about his divorce, was doing nothing more with his pieces than venting and letting off steam. I was not the least bit touched by his divorce, nor was I offered truths that illuminated my life. Either Dave did not learn anything from his experience or he could not communicate his revelation.

While anger was admittedly one of the feelings that came out in my essay "Waiting for Daddy" and in all my subsequent pieces about my divorce, I like to think I moved through it toward some wisdom or understanding, arriving at the truth, which is the advice offered to me by a friend, that "the pain never goes away so you have to start moving and working with it." In "20 Things I Learned Since My Marriage Ended" (*Cosmopolitan*, November 1984), besides discovering certain things such as the gas tank is on the right side of the car, I *can* parallel park my car in a very tight spot, nothing ever turns out as planned and it is virtually impossible to have a relationship with a picky eater, I learned that not too much in life really matters if we don't first and foremost have ourselves.

In "My Inner Shrimp" (Sunday *New York Times Magazine*, March 31, 1996), Garry Trudeau wrote about the hell he endured growing up short. He didn't just voice his complaints about it, though. He came out the other end.

Tall.

And with a wonderful, wonderful truth about adolescent hierarchies and how they endure. Trudeau still sees himself as a midget. That is who he is in his mind.

That is a truth most of us share: No matter what we become or do in later life, we tend to always see ourselves as we (and they) did when we were young. Trudeau writes:

> In my 17th year, I miraculously shot up six inches, just in time for graduation and a fresh start. I was, in the space of a few months, reborn—and I made the most of it. Which is to say that thereafter, all of life's disappointments, reversals and calamities still arrived on

schedule—but blissfully free of subtext . . .

And yet the impact of being literally looked down on, of being made to feel small, is forever. It teaches you how to stretch, how to survive the scorn of others for things beyond your control. Not growing forces you to grow up fast.

Notice how the three components—a point of view, emotional involvement and the arrival at a basic truth—were all there in Trudeau's "My Inner Shrimp."

All three components are clearly required.

If those are there, you can whine and kvetch, because clearly you are doing more.

$\mathcal{E}$*xercise*

Think about what you looked like as an adolescent. Did you have some physical attribute that set you apart from the clique? Were you too short? Too tall? Too fat? Too something?

Write about it using dramatic scenes with dialogue and action to capture what you went through. Your self-consciousness and pain may have been heavy, but your tone needn't be.

SHOW DON'T TELL

We are back to word pictures. To emotional involvement. To what I call "going into the world" or "putting yourself at the heart of the scene" or "taking the reader right there."

No matter what anyone calls it, it is all about *show, don't tell*.

If this is the first time you have heard show, don't tell, you are either very, very new to writing or residing somewhere near the moon. It is among the most valuable lessons of any writing book or class or teacher. It is among the most important things you do. My students who never heard me say "show, don't tell" either dropped my course after eleven minutes or are in a deep psychotic state.

Showing is acting on paper. Moment to moment in the scene. The curtain goes up on a brightly lit stage and you are right there at the center.

In her *Times* Op-Ed piece, "They Don't Take Just Any Mutt," which we discussed a few sections earlier, my student Michele *shows* us what she went through getting her two golden retrievers into a New York City dog run through conversations with other humans, and with her two dogs, Willi and Dune:

> "I'll put you on the waiting list," said a woman who answered the phone at the dog run. Waiting list? Had I reached N.Y.U. admissions by mistake? . . . . Weeks passed without a word. When we walked by the run, Willi and Dune barked at the dogs inside. "You're just as good as they are," I said, consolingly.
>
> Six months later, I came home to a message that an application was in the mail. I shook the dogs awake.
>
> "You're in, you made it," I cried, too caught up to realize that they hadn't dwelled on this for months.

When you write a scene, put yourself and the people or pets to whom you are speaking at the center of the stage.

Talk to them.

Do something with or to them.

Show you and them react.

In previous sections, I shared and analyzed scenes from my published work: one of my older sister and me in the backseat of the car, another of me on a lounge chair watching my daughter and father swim, and still another of my daughter in the lobby of our apartment building where her father will pick her up.

In all of these, I tried to convey where I stood and what I

was about. I was saying: This is where I am. Now I am going to show you what I went through and what it was like. Wanna come?

In an essay called "My Mostly Companion," which appeared as a Hers column in the Sunday *Times Magazine* (June 13, 1993), I show the agony and ecstasy of a bathing suit shopping excursion with my daughter who was fifteen at the time:

> As we got off the escalator at the trauma department, my eyes were caught immediately by a chic, moderately revealing, black-and-white-check bathing suit. I took it off the rack to admire, then quickly put it back.
>
> My daughter, already holding several bikinis in size 3 and 5, turned to me.
>
> "Why'd you do that?"
>
> I shrugged.
>
> "What about 'Trust your gut,' Ma?"
>
> I glanced at the checked suit. "It doesn't have a skirt."
>
> She rolled her eyes towards heaven and told me to get real.
>
> Between us we took forty-some bathing suits (including the black-and-white check, in two sizes), two at a time, into one fitting room, then spread out into two booths. We went back and forth for each other's opinions, assessing our own and the other's figures, alternately laughing and complaining.
>
> My daughter wished she looked curvier in bikinis. I wished I looked like my daughter. Her misery was more palpable than mine, though. Decades of bathing suit shopping had numbed me.
>
> "That looks good on you," she said as I tried on the black-and-white check.
>
> It did, surprisingly. It was different from anything I had ever tried. Or owned. I was pleased.

No. Not pleased. I was actually ecstatic. I can't remember ever thinking I looked good in a bathing suit or better than my daughter—a size 2. That was a first. And her compliment "that looks good on you" added complications. A validation. And a sharp pang of guilt. Our children are supposed to have it better than we do. Even in bathing suits.

There was no way I could comfortably wear that black-and-white-check bathing suit let alone buy it if we didn't find a great suit for her.

> I put on my street clothes, went out to the racks, and took one last look around, finding—thank God—a really pretty bikini.
>
> I grabbed it and rushed to the fitting room.
>
> "It's you," I said. "Don't you think?"
>
> Her eyes lit up, but just a little. I waited outside the fitting room while she tried it on, taking slow deep breaths and praying.
>
> When she opened the curtain, she was smiling. And admiring herself from all sides. Rightfully so. She looked terrific.
>
> Bingo!
>
> "That wasn't so bad," she said as we left the store with our two bags. Not so bad? What about her agony the first hour and a half? Or my ecstasy in a bathing suit I never would have chosen on my own?
>
> "No it wasn't," I said. We got on the bus and rode home contentedly, Sisters in bathing suit heaven.

Reliving on paper

The tension I felt in the trauma department rushing into the fitting room with that bikini was there again when I wrote that scene. It was in my stomach. In every pore. And every word. That bikini was my hope.

And what a relief when she liked it. It made mother and daughter great friends.

I felt this experience deeply. And again when I committed it to the page. Every emotion I ever felt with and for my daughter came alive in the trauma department that day. When I relived them on paper, I had us talking, acting and reacting to dramatize these emotions and show the complexity of our bond.

Let's return now to a master, Russell Baker, and the beginning of his second memoir, *Good Times*:

> My mother, dead now to this world but still roaming free in my mind, wakes me some mornings before daybreak. "If there's one thing I can't stand, it's a quitter."
> I heard her say that all my life. Now, lying in bed, coming awake in the dark, I feel the fury of her energy fighting the good-for-nothing idler within me who wants to go back to sleep instead of tackling the brave new day.

How does Baker pull the reader in here?

For starters, look at that first sentence. It's not only funny, but true. Don't we all hear our mothers throughout our whole lives wherever they or we happen to be?

That image of his mother waking him is fresh. It's unusually worded. Baker turns a phrase so well. And again the voice is so likable and warm.

Then in the next sentence he makes us hear his mother's voice. And listen to what she says. She can't stand a quitter. And she is not letting him off the hook. This is even funnier and fresher with a powerful ring of truth. If you did not have a mother who hounded you to achieve, surely some other adult in your life gave you a kick or push.

Baker's opening would not have been as compelling had he started with something like, "My mother was a strong influence."

He dramatized through very funny words and actions just how she held the reins.

Showing means putting yourself there. Right there.

Don't describe the experience. Or explain the event. Relive it on paper by going back into it yourself.

Choosing details

As you think of experiences you wish to write about, recall the images that first come to mind. What details are still most vivid? Jot down those that still bring a lump to your throat. Or make you giggle. Or cringe. Or gasp. Or react in some other way.

Think, too, of the people who were there. What did they do? And say? Jot down their actions and dialogue.

Continue to brainstorm and freewrite.

Let's close with Baker's last scene of *Good Times*. It is the day of his mother's funeral.

> I was aware of my life stretching across a great expanse of time, of reaching across some two hundred years inside this old house and connecting Ida Rebecca's Civil War America with whatever America might be in the middle of the twenty-first century.
>
> My father's funeral procession had set out from another house just up the road from this one. Thirty-three he was at death. And now my daughter, Kathy, was thirty-two, my son Allen thirty-one, my son Michael twenty-nine.
>
> Looking at them grouped with Audrey's children around the fireplace, I realized that if my father were mysteriously compelled to join us this day, he would gravitate naturally to my children for the companionship of his own kind. If he noticed me staring too curiously at him, he might turn to Kathy or Allen or Michael and whisper, asking, "Who's the old man in the high-priced suit?"
>
> I was now old enough to be his father.
>
> So it is with a family. We carry the dead generations

within us and pass them on to the future aboard our children. This keeps the people of the past alive long after we have taken them to the churchyard.

"If there's one thing I can't stand, Russell, it's a quitter."

Lord, I can hear her still.

And so now probably can you.

The memory is poignant. Baker goes inside himself as he is standing there. And with great warmth, and humanity, he shares his memories, feelings, the imagined words of his long-deceased father and again the very loud, clear ones of his mother that implode on our memories long after we finish the book.

Images, specific details, good truths and insights coupled with voices—one booming through these pages and his life—are given to us with immediacy and simplicity.

In Baker's perfect pitch.

Exercise

Think about a memorable past or present experience from your life. Pretend you are on a brightly lit stage with the curtain opening. Put yourself at the center of the experience again. Relive it. Make sure you are fully there.

Bring it to us on paper by *showing*, not telling what you went through. See it the way you did then, using the details, voices and actions.

Dramatize! Dramatize! Dramatize!

SHOW. YES SHOW! JUST NOT EVERYTHING

So now you are showing, not telling.

It gets easier the more you write. Do the exercises. Again and again. Be willing to keep opening up.

And be willing, too, to leave some things out. Your writing is not a cure for insomnia. You don't want to put readers off. No one can stand an old windbag. In person. Or in print.

So unless it is essential to the story and to the point you are driving home, do not include what you ate for every meal during your six-week stay in Capri. Leave out the foods that did not agree. Everyone eats and digests. If nothing weird happened when you ate pasta and bread, it's best you leave that out.

Omit how many and which buses you take to work. Do not share the details of the traffic. Most of us use transportation regularly. No one cares. Unless you are traveling by stagecoach, or carpooling with the Ku Klux Klan.

Remember: Reading is not watching television. It is a far more active pursuit. You want to move, inform and enlighten your readers. You want them to be fully engaged.

Show your turmoil. Your strife. What is going on between you and your mate. You and those family members with whom you have battled or struggled. Or the conflicts between you and you.

That is what readers are after. The truths about life and themselves illuminated through a journey that touches their hearts and souls. Your trailing them from Macy's to Nordstroms to The Gap and then to that cute little new boutique will not do that anymore than will the contents of your last low-sodium meal.

Author Mary McGarry Morris opens her novel *Vanished* with a ten-page prologue, then goes on to chapter one, which begins like this:

> Five years passed. And maybe a million miles. He was caught and he knew it, caught in a dream or a nightmare or one of Hyacinth's stories, and there seemed no way out of anything anymore, certainly no way of his choosing. Even though he had come to love the little girl they called Canny, he continued to miss his sons.

The first two sentences make me wonder if in early drafts, Morris had one to several chapters about what happened during those five years and million miles and then saw or had it pointed out by an editor that what she wrote was neither pertinent nor relevant nor dramatic enough to leave in.

We will never know, but "Five years passed. And maybe a million miles" works fine. I don't need anything more.

Years ago, I had a piece in the travel section of the *Times* about my experiences in a group beach house on Fire Island. Eight people with quarter- and half-shares spent summer weekends there. In my first few drafts, I had all eight of us trailing through every weekend. Between those and my final drafts, I turned the eight of us into six, compiled our most interesting traits, and eliminated details and ho-hum weekends that didn't move my story along or illuminate what I arrived at:

- that we take ourselves with us wherever we go,
- that living with other people is hard,
- that despite the stress and tension, we need one another so we learn how to compromise and adjust.

Eight people had made the piece unwieldy. Our sunny, conflict-free weekends had no subtext. To show our mounting tension, I used only rainy weekends or those when we had guests. My first draft was thirteen manuscript pages. My final draft was five.

Unless they are essential to the point you are driving home, do not include your every movement, moment, weekend or conversation. Leave out some people, too.

And leave out the mundane details: how many streets you crossed to reach your destination and how many stores you searched before finding the mauve scarf.

To justify such inclusions, students often tell me, "But that really happened," to which I respond, "So what?" When I tell them to write about an experience that affected them, I suggest they begin the pieces *after breakfast*: Unless they found rubies in their western omelet, choked on a piece of eggshell or fell in love over the whole wheat toast, no one cares what they ate or said with their morning cup of coffee.

How do you know the difference between what is compelling and ho-hum?

You don't always.

At least not in the beginning. It takes writing. And weeding things out.

If something in your experience obsesses you and lights your fire, there is a good reason. And if it doesn't turn you on at all or haunt you in any way, that's a tip-off, too.

Advice

Look back at the exercises you have done so far. Is there anything in them that is not even exciting to you?

Any details? Conversations that go nowhere? Information that unless you are writing a factual report is flat or boring or mundane?

If you have used anything that is putting you to sleep, just imagine what it might do to readers.

Trust your gut reactions. They may be physical. And catch you unaware. Does your work charge you up? Make you more conscious and alive? Or make you wish you were somewhere else?

Note in the exercises you have done so far if your scenes have tension, emotional turmoil and something going on between the lines.

Exercise

Take one of your pieces and eliminate the details, conversations, adjectives and information that are not fresh, do not show tension or reveal anything about you. Rewrite the piece without them.

REVEAL YOURSELF HONESTLY

Courage.

Like taking Frost's less traveled road, having courage makes all the difference. That is what good writing is about.

Tell the truth. Be yourself on the page. Let it roll, baby. Let it roll.

Pretend you're in high school and in your bedroom alone with your favorite rock music blasting. Boogie on paper like you boogied back then when no one was around.

Good writing is about letting go. It's about losing your self-consciousness. It leads you to your truest self. And to enormous possibility.

I have often been asked how I have the nerve to write about certain things for publication. "A New Mother's Confessions of Ambivalence" was my first personal experience piece to elicit this sort of question. In it, I shared my frustrations and fears, capturing the darker side of motherhood.

This was also the first of my published personal essays that generated lots of mail. Mothers expressed their gratitude. They told me I understood how they felt. Editors of magazines invited me to submit my future personal writing to them.

Admittedly, I was thrilled by the response. I liked knowing I touched a few hearts. I wasn't nearly as thrilled as I had been, though, when I had let go and expressed what I felt.

It was a freedom I had never experienced with the pieces I'd written before.

You want that kind of freedom, too. To feel as if Someone Up There is giving you dictation and saying, "Go ahead now. Move your pen."

The more you write, the more that happens. You keep chiseling and chiseling away. Yes, it is scary to face the blank page and ourselves. Scary to face The Truth.

The only thing scarier is not to.

How can you tell when you are hitting on something, getting to your truths?

First, your body may react. Your heart may start beating faster. You may feel a kink in your shoulders or neck. Or get a knot or butterflies in your stomach. Or break out in hives. Or a sweat.

And you may very well start to cry.

You may also bolt. Just leave the room. The intensity you brought on is too much.

I know when I am hitting on something: I bounce up and go to the fridge.

I cool off or pig out. Sometimes both. Then I walk around my apartment. I comb my hair. Talk to myself. Check the mail.

Go back to the fridge. A few minutes and too many calories later, I invariably return to my work.

Yes, that first jolt of the truth sends me running, but then I come right back.

My answer to those who ask how I can say certain things in print is this:

It is what I do. It is who I am. And even though it sometimes freaks me out, for me it sure beats hiding.

You have your reasons for writing. I hope one is that you want to write. If you do, then it helps to face reality. Whatever your reality is.

Turning your experiences into words takes courage and a willingness to let people see who you are.

I pulverize students who don't show themselves. I'm on their case when they try to hide. As one whom I regularly hound put it, "You only like a certain kind of writer."

C'est vrai. The kind who tells the truth.

Exercise

Think of a time when you needed courage. It can be a scary piano recital, your wedding, facing an illness, facing your ex, your first day of school or camp, your first sleepover, your first anything.

Write about it showing what you did and how you used your courage.

CHAPTER SEVENTEEN

Writing About "Nots"

I'm not as normal as I appear.
—Woody Allen

O ne of the first pieces I had published in *New Woman* was a personal essay called "On Not Looking Like Catherine Deneuve." The impetus was a television commercial for Chanel perfume. It starred Catherine and a bottle. In a seductive pose, she appeared on the screen, luring homeviewers into buying the product. She hadn't come into our homes occasionally, either. Nuh-uh. For a long time, the fabulous-looking star was in our faces as many evenings a week as Dan Rather.

That commercial and the image got me. Got me between the eyes. It sparked deeply buried feelings. One day I wrote this lead:

> Several years ago, it seemed that whenever I turned on my television, Catherine Deneuve was reclining by a bottle of perfume. With her head slightly tilted and her

long, blond mane draped over her shoulders, she would gaze into my living room and say, with great earnestness, and in that lovely French accent, "Do you think it is easy being Catherine Deneuve?"

I would look back at that face, and in my American accent, and with even greater earnestness answer, "Yes, Catherine. I do."

I mean, really. Who was she kidding?

Not me, baby. Not me at all. My feelings about chiseled beauty started pouring out on the page. Having Catherine Deneuve ask millions of homeviewers who look nothing like her and don't even come close if we think it is easy being her was among the most absurd questions ever asked.

What is easier?

You know what else?

I think that when Catherine is doing anything but reclining by a perfume bottle, she thinks it is easy too. Otherwise she would have written a personal experience piece about what she has gone through not looking like me.

One of the reasons writers write is to make sense of what we are not. Or do not have. We look at what is off, or missing, or out of kilter and try to understand it. What is our place on this planet, we ask ourselves. How do we fit in?

Writing is an act of discovery. It is a way to figure things out. When you write, you learn something about yourself. If you don't, there is no deal.

THE ROLE OF CONFLICT

Start with your question. Or struggle. Whatever you are not. Or don't have. Write about those fundamental conflicts that keep your therapist nodding. Or about your conflicts here and now.

In her essay "City Kid" (*Living Aloud*, Random House), Anna Quindlen wrote about how she came to the decision not to move to the suburbs despite its obvious advantages for her children. She shares her conflict. In the suburbs, the schools are better. There is more grass. More space. It is easier for the children to play outside. But then she writes that they "will play with other kids who are just like them, on streets that are just like ours and just like the one where I played with kids just like me."

And when her closest friend, a city person too, moves to a suburb and loves it for its peace and quiet, Quindlen sums up why she cannot move—she finds the suburbs deadening—bringing the reader to her decision to stay put, ending with the following take on her friend's assessment: "Exactly. That's my problem right there."

My student who is a minister sold a personal essay to *Parents* about his conflict the Christmas Eve his wife went into labor and he had to be in church. He took us to the hospital during the delivery and his fretting about the midnight mass, the puppet show, which won't go smoothly without him. Eventually he sees where he belongs and wants to be: exactly where he is at the moment with his wife and brand new son.

Michele, my student, would never have written "Hunting for a New Therapist" if the therapist she had been seeing was not so far away. And she would not have had to keep hunting if the first one she consulted was sane. Of course, Michele would never have been in the market for a therapist in the first place had she felt all her ducks were in line.

In Nora Ephron's delightful essay "A Few Words About Breasts," she chronicles her experiences growing up with small ones. As the girls in her class were developing and nothing was happening to her, she tells her mother "I want a bra" on more than one occasion. Each time her mother says, "What for?"

At nineteen, her boyfriend's mother asked her if she thought they would get married. When she said "yes," here was the woman's response:

"Fine . . . Now, here's what you do. Always make sure you're on top of him so you won't seem so small."

Ephron then shares several experiences she had with men, revealing her discomfort, and a string of remarks women have made to her about breast size. The voluptuous ones regularly assured her their problems were far worse than hers. But if growing up with small breasts had given her great joy, she wouldn't have had an essay's worth of material. Not even a few words.

And had Garry Trudeau been tall as a boy, he would not have written "My Inner Shrimp." And Allan Ishac, whose piece we discussed in an earlier section, would never have written "A Son's Vigil" had his father not been so old.

THE BAD NEWS IS GOOD NEWS

You have big-time "nots." And little "nots." Use them. They are your material. They are stuff about which you should write.

I have written about my less-than-perfect relationships and my less-than-perfect thighs. The former was the subject of an entire book and numerous essays. The latter became a short piece I called "On No Longer Being Size 5."

Certainly you have had struggles. With your weight. Relationships. Work. On trips.

One of my early published pieces, "Travels With a Novice," was about my first trip to Europe. I schlepped through nine countries in less than eight weeks with a foul-mouthed, mean-spirited girl who was also promiscuous, obese and cheap.

Had she and I gotten along famously and had the trip been la-de-da, I would have had only three words about the experience: Everything was good.

I got several essays out of my migraines as an elementary school teacher. The first, "An Apple for My Children," was about a disastrous class trip to the Museum of Natural History on which no one heard a single word I said except the boy who yelled, "Cut the shit, shorty." Another was about learning to connect with a girl who tested me daily. Had she been goody-two-shoes and not a problem, there would have been nothing to write.

If your job is totally devoid of stress and your relationships are loving and sane, take a look at whatever else in your life has caused or is causing you pain.

The good news is *nothing bad happens to a writer.*

Bad is often good.

No one has the answers. When you sort through your personal struggles on paper, you hit readers where they live.

Sharon, my student with ovarian cancer, wrote about what she went through the first time she wore a wig. It was to a party at the Museum of Modern Art where everyone she spoke to was nauseatingly chic. Their comments on her new "do" combined with Sharon's sardonic take made for one helluva touching piece.

"It's terrific," another student told her the night it was read aloud. "How do you do it?"

"Cancer," Sharon said.

In a television interview, director Sidney Pollack was discussing "The Way We Were." He said there were only a few minutes in the entire movie in which Robert Redford and Barbra Streisand got along. What could there possibly be to say, to dramatize, if they spent two hours on the beach arm in arm?

So if you are struggling with love, with work, with your family, be thankful. Your misery will help move your pen. And if you are not, don't sweat it. You can find plenty in your life out of whack.

As a writer, give thanks for your misery. And for whatever you are "not."

Exercise

Write about something (or someone) with which you have struggled. Make sure you tell the truth.

CHAPTER EIGHTEEN

Everyone Can Hear the Music

*The first prerogative of an artist in any medium is to make
a fool of himself.*

—Pauline Kael

I am new at using my body. I was raised to use my mind.
My family is "mental." Very mental, indeed.

Growing up, I got points for head stuff. I scored big-
time when I had clever retorts. The validation for my "mental-
ness" was appreciated and nourishing, but it was easier to sit
than to move. I did not get the hang of grooving. I was far too
self-conscious to boogey anywhere outside my room.

A few years ago, I was vacationing at a spa and took a class
called Funky Aerobics. The instructor was surprisingly young
and sexy in a streetlike way. Unlike the others who taught there,
she wasn't in gym shorts or sweats. She wore a black tanktop with
tight cutoff jeans. And boy could she ever move! She bumped and
grinded and gyrated like she'd been doing it her whole life.

Such a cool chick, I thought. She made it fun to watch and do. I was all the way in the back hoping no one would see me klutzing around.

Only I didn't.

Maybe because I didn't know anyone or because I was among the younger guests and more had stretch marks than not, I was feeling the beat and moving more freely than I ever thought I could.

"Uh-huh. You got it! You can be funky, too," the teacher said.

I did. And I was. Perhaps I was dreaming, but with each one of her "you got its," her eyes were right on me. By the time the class was over, I was almost cool, too.

Funky Aerobics was offered the next day and taught again by her. This time I was in the front row, following her every move. When she said, "Uh-huh. You got it," I knew she was looking at me. I was letting it go. And looser yet. And more and more in the groove.

When the class was over, I went up to thank her for a totally terrific time.

"Your sexiness is contagious," I told her. "Were you born that way?"

She burst out laughing, then grabbed my elbow and pulled me over to the walk-in closet where she had to turn off the music and no one else was around.

"I just got this way yesterday," she whispered.

Huh?

She went on. "The regular teacher quit and this is the most popular class here. I was the only one free at the hour so I had to get funky. And fast." She leaned in closer. "I'm not funky. I'm an athlete."

An hour later I saw her again in white tennis shorts and a T-shirt on the tennis court. She was teaching the forehand to a couple, instructing them to "follow through."

She looked incredibly athletic. Not unlike our Billie Jean. It was hard to believe that just an hour and an outfit ago, she had been a cool chick and in the groove.

Everyone hears the music. Everyone can dance.

You have to want to do it.

And be willing to take risks. To be funky, to write, to have fun doing anything, you have to give yourself permission to make a fool of yourself.

No one gets anywhere playing it safe.

Writing, like funky aerobics, is about loosening up and letting go. It means relaxing and trusting and being able to lose yourself and lose control.

Find a comfortable place to write. Physically and within yourself.

"Uh-huh. You got it! You can be funky, too."

Advice

Recall the labels you were given as a child and in your more recent past. How did they help or hinder you? Think of specific ways they left a mark.

Exercise

Jot down everything you recall about your labels and write about their impact.

Now write another piece totally uncharacteristic of you. Use a tone, approach and style that is very different for you.

CHAPTER NINETEEN

Being Somewhere Else: Getting Ideas

We try not to have ideas, preferring accidents. To create,
you must empty yourself of every artistic thought.
—Gilbert Proesch

We often get our best ideas when we are somewhere else.

Somewhere *far* from our desk and computer when we are not sitting there *trying* to work. It's simple. And remarkable. And at times, I think, perverse. Ideas, like love and most good things, appear when we least expect them, not when we demand they should.

It helps to *not* be looking, but to be in the throes of life. That's when ideas quietly tap us. Or hit us between the eyes. Or tickle or scratch or itch us. Or sneak right up from behind.

My friend Tom McKean, the young adult novelist, was talking to a colleague who made a nasty comment. He took it as a put-down and told her he was insulted. She said she meant no harm adding, "That wasn't me talking. It was my evil twin."

Evil twin! What a concept! Her comment put a gleam in Tom's eye. A child could do and say whatever he wished, Tom thought, if he attributes the behavior to a twin.

Wheels turned. Tom had a premise. A boy pretends to be twins. Tom wrote a novel called *My Evil Twin*.

At the time, Tom was not looking for an idea. He had another book in the works. But fortunately a colleague made a stupid comment. And fortunately she apologized with more to say than "sorry."

And fortunately Tom grabbed that "more" and turned it into a novel.

How did Tom know an idea when he heard it?

He didn't. He is a writer. Something got him going. A colleague uttered two sentences and Tom caucused with his muse.

Writers are always working—always writing—whether they are putting words down or not. Something hits or nudges or amuses or bothers us as we go about living our lives.

It can happen in conversations. In the produce department. Or in meats. At the gym. Or in the shower. It can happen crossing the street.

You hear a comment that reminds you of a childhood incident. You run into a foe or friend. Someone in your office gets pregnant. Or fired. Something sparks you. You run for your pen.

In Ralph Waldo Emerson's essay on self-reliance, he says:

> A man should learn to detect that gleam of light which flashes across his mind from within, more than the luster of the firmament of bards and sages. Yet he dismisses without notice his thought, because it is his. In every work of genius we recognize our own rejected thoughts.

Playwright Neil Simon was not at his typewriter when he got the premise for *Barefoot in the Park*. He was arguing with his wife in the kitchen. And ducking. She'd just thrown a veal chop at him.

My student Doris got an idea at the beauty parlor looking at her new do. She thought it made her look matronly and even older than her mother. That concept sparked her. Buried feelings began to emerge. Doris took out a pen and paper and began writing on the bus ride home.

My student Michele, whom we discussed earlier, came to class each week describing what it was like getting her dogs accepted to a dog run. It was a New York story through and through. And worse than getting into college. We suggested she write about it, which she did. And she published it in the *Times*.

TRUST THE GLEAM IN YOUR EYE

Often my students arrive at class with ideas. They are fired up to write. They tell me about something they saw or heard. Does it sound like a good idea?

Anything is good if it grabs or sparks the writer. My antenna may not be out there for a line about an evil twin. But it picks up images I see on walks. And interactions between parents and children.

An idea came to me one evening when I was walking by a neighborhood church. The AA meeting was over. OA was about to begin. I went home and wrote an essay about not having any anonymouses.

Another idea came to me at ten one night in the kitchen of my daughter's friend. I had come to pick up my daughter, and the other mother, who had just gotten home, was having a bird and a half:

> The salad she had made for them was still in the refrigerator. The girls claimed they hadn't seen it. She insisted they eat it. As they stood silently together, leaning against the kitchen counter and crunching on the vegetables, my daughter glanced in my direction, rolling her eyes towards heaven. Her friend, no longer able to take

it, stormed out of the apartment. After my daughter took her last forkful, she and I quietly left.

But not before she politely thanked the mother for dinner.

In the next scene of the piece, my daughter and I are laughing at what just happened as we walk home arm in arm and I know that at any minute—she is a teenager and I am human—everything could change.

I was struck with the idea for "My Mostly Companion," which I discussed in an earlier section, while I was in the bathing suit department of Lord & Taylor. I got another at my parents' pool. And still another in the auditorium of the High School of Performing Arts after my daughter had an audition.

When you are elsewhere and get an idea, it may not come full blown. It's more like an itch or a poke. You don't have to know then if it will be a piece. Or how it fits into one.

Learn to trust that gleam in your eye whether it comes at the beauty parlor or at work. There is a reason an idea comes to you. Play with it. Use it. It is yours.

How do you know if the idea you get from an image or conversation or incident is material you can shape into an entire piece?

You don't.

But you do know when it elicits strong reactions. You know when you are grabbed. You might giggle or sweat or breathe faster or scream. Then it will sit with you, obsess you and play over many times in your mind.

That is reason enough to write about it.

In the process you will figure it out.

Sometimes, and this often happens to me, the experiences that stir and touch and tickle you are not always an entire piece. Bathing suit shopping, for example, was just a part of something larger.

Take mental notes. Take physical notes. Use them. Pay attention.

Most of our writing gets done when we don't seem to be writing at all. As Ralph Waldo Emerson wrote:

> For, often, don't you—when you're starting out to write something—dismiss without notice, a thought because it is merely yours. You get just this split second side glimpse, a tantalizing flash of wings, before you reject it categorically. "No," you say, "that couldn't have been a swallow—much less an angel. . . ." And you return to your glumness and panic and low opinion of yourself.

Advice

Entertain your ideas, not your critics. They can fend for themselves.

Trust what stirs you.

Don't second-guess yourself.

Your first impulse is your creative stuff, your child, your true self.

More Advice

Don't worry if you are not blown away or dazzled or struck down. Your ideas may hit you in dribbles and spurts and rushes and ripples and waves. If you can't use them right away, let them simmer, let them stew. Whatever they are and however they appear, *don't dismiss them or throw them away.*

Not every idea is a winner. And neither is every guy. You don't know if something is right from a distance. Get your feet wet and try.

Things to Do

Keep a pad in your purse or pocket wherever you go. See yourself as Harriet or Harry the Spy.

Keep a pad near your bed.

Pay attention to what you hear around you: at work, with your family, at meals, on the bus.

Jot down the things that get you and obsess you. They are yours.

Exercise

Write about something a spouse or love or ex has said to you that evoked a strong reaction.

CHAPTER TWENTY

One True Thing

If you do not tell the truth about yourself you cannot tell it about other people.

—*Virginia Woolf*

I taught a four-session afternoon writing workshop at N.Y.U. that began on February 13. At the first session, I had my students write about a memorable Valentine's Day. After fifteen minutes I stopped them to discuss how they were doing. Those who spoke said they were doing fine and were eager to write more.

For their home assignment due the following week, they were to finish two pages on Valentine's Day, or write about another holiday—any holiday—that was memorable. At the beginning of the second session, I asked them how it went.

A grim-looking woman sitting right in front of me immediately raised her hand. "Terrible," she said. "I hate holidays. I always did. I couldn't even think of one that had any meaning. So I really didn't do what you wanted."

Uh-huh.

I read my students' work aloud anonymously, and as soon as

I began our curmudgeon's, everyone knew whose it was. She took us right to Thanksgiving dinner with her dysfunctional, non-communicative family, to Christmas with the same crew, then to several rotten New Year's Eves when she was alone, or with some jerk, or asleep.

My other students and I were howling. Howling with delight. Her romp through holiday hell was hilarious. Of course, we've been there ourselves.

Then from her darkest New Year's Eve, she took us to her real holiday, Every Day, and to her present dinner table where she eats with her husband and two children laughing, planning and sharing what they each had done that day.

My students were nodding. I was too. A familiar lump formed in my throat. The lump I cannot prevent from forming whenever I am touched by something real.

"It's great," I told my holiday hater.

She looked a tad surprised. "It wasn't what you wanted."

"Better," I told her and the class. "You were honest. It was your truth."

In her novel *A Mother and Two Daughters*, Gail Godwin's character Lydia Strickland Mansfield, a woman in her late thirties, has just returned to college and is struggling with a term paper.

> She read over what she had written. It flowed nicely, but was it a little too glib? Did it fall too much into the currently popular ruts of blame? ("Look what a mess we're in because they told us lies.") But how else should she start? She looked at her watch and realized she had wasted almost an hour getting started. She began to panic, as she used to, long ago, whenever she had to write a book report for school. One night she had worked herself into hysterics because she couldn't get the first sentence of her book report. Daddy had taken her downstairs to his study and sat her down on his leather sofa

with a sharp pencil and one of his brand-new legal pads. "Now all you have to do is write me down one true thing about that book," Daddy said. "I haven't read it, so anything you can tell me about it will be of interest. Don't think of what your teacher expects you to write, or what you think you should write. Just write down one true thing about that book."

So never mind what I expect or what you think you should write. The deal is to tell the truth.

Holidays were the pits for my student. Simple daily moments are real. She got to it. She told the truth. And hit us where we live.

Except for plot-driven books or escapist fiction, I believe all writing, to be good let alone great, must be self-revelatory. Truthful. And sincere.

That means putting yourself on the page. Your self that may loathe forced celebrations. And finds the joy in Every Day.

One of the reasons we write is to find out our truths. To make sense of our world, and what we think and feel. Or as Gail Godwin put it:

> To better understand who and what we are and in what kind of place we're actually living. Built from our own observations: not secondhand ones.

The world according to my holiday hater isn't the world according to you. Be yourself in whatever you write. Make sure you tell the truth.

Exercise

From your own observations, feelings and experiences, write about something you hate. It can be a holiday, doing assignments or anything you want.

Write one true thing about it. *Your* true thing.

CHAPTER TWENTY-ONE

Write What You Know

A man travels the world over in search of what he needs and returns home to find it.

—George Moore

You needn't schlep to the Himalayas for material. That is not what good writing is about. Jane Austen was not a Frequent Flyer. The Brontës rarely left home.

Start with yourself. Look at your life. See what's missing and what is there. Look at your family. At your struggles and triumphs. Look at how and where you fit in.

Writer Gloria Naylor said with her first novel, *The Women of Brewster Place*, she was "going to write about what I had not, in those twenty-some years of literacy, the privilege to read about, I was going to write about me."

As Naylor puts it:

> You write from where you are. It's the only thing you have to give. And if you are fortunate enough, there is

a spark that will somehow ignite a work so that it touches almost anyone who reads it. . . . Every writer must articulate from the specific. They write from where they stand, because there is nothing else from which to draw.

I was raised in Buffalo, New York, so what I knew was snow. At seven years old, I looked out my window and this was what I wrote:

> The other night when I saw snow
> I knew our car would not go.
> From my window it looked so bright
> It was really a beautiful sight
> So I played and played on my sled
> Until my mother called me to go to bed.

Not exactly Robert Frost. Not even Michael Fein. He was, according to our teacher and the principal, the poet of the second grade.

But I got a kick out of sitting in my room putting my thoughts into words. And that's even truer today.

I don't leave New York to find material. I rarely leave my block. Writing isn't about going far. It's about going far within.

LOOK INSIDE

You've had quiet moments with your family and friends. Probably some noisy ones, too. You've had moments when you look out your window at the street or in your yard. Write about what these moments mean.

You have a self. And a wellspring of experiences. You have relationships, emotions and a life. There've been people who have loved and pulverzied you. Put them on the page.

Have you overcome a handicap? Or do you live with someone who did? Do you have children? Why? Or why not? These are evergreens.

You are not required to travel the world. Or have a wild and crazy life. You can mine what is near. And dear or not. You can write about a Christmas. Or snow.

All experiences are material. It is about what you have to say.

Eudora Welty says it perfectly in the last paragraph of her autobiography, *One Writer's Beginnings*:

> As you have seen, I am a writer who came from a sheltered life. A sheltered life can be a daring life as well. For all serious daring starts from within.

Exercise

Write about a daring personal experience. An experience in which you had to stretch yourself, call upon inner resources and grow. It can be anything from giving a speech, being in the school play, standing up for yourself, moving to another city, taking a new job or owning up to something you did.

Use specific details to capture your feelings, the place and the struggle.

CHAPTER TWENTY-TWO

Keeping a Journal

I never travel without my diary. One should always have
something sensational to read on the train.
   —*Oscar Wilde*

*I*f you do not already keep a journal, this is a good time to start. It need not have the word "journal" or precious, wide-eyed kittens. Write in whatever kind you like. A spiral notebook will do.

What goes in them? There are no shoulds. You can fill it with anything: ideas, observations, overheard conversations, longings, phrases and musings.

To get you started or keep you going, consider the following suggestions.

BE CONSISTENT

Write down your fears, dreams, feelings, experiences and thoughts regularly. Do this even when you are not dying to do so or when you think you have nothing to say.

You may hit on something you wish to use elsewhere. You won't know unless you show up. And much of the time if you keep your pen moving, your muse will decide to kick in.

If what you say in your journal remains between you and you, that is terrific too. By writing in it, you become more awake and conscious. Not such bad things to be.

There are two ways to become a better writer:

1. By writing
2. By becoming increasingly self-aware

If you think you are sounding crazy or silly, all the more reason to say it. That is your stuff. Yours alone. And probably your truest self. Keep it going. Keep it alive. And let it all hang out. No one will cart you to the loony bin when you write your truths for yourself.

You may be in a rut at work. Or overwhelmed with demands at home. Or maybe you're in a domestic rut. And overwhelmed by the demands of your boss.

Having a journal in which to contemplate your experiences is reason enough to keep one. If something more evolves from that, consider it a benefit.

EXPLORE DEMONS AND SECRETS

Write in your journal when you are absolutely burning to get something off your chest or have a strong need to express your feelings.

What better outlet is there for your secrets and demons than in a safe place no one can see?

You can write about the family alcoholic. Or about the athlete. Or the one who is certifiably nuts. You can write what it's like—really like—being with them. And what it puts you through.

You can write about death and what it was like losing your aunt or your cocker spaniel. Or about the death of a long-term relationship. Maybe your closest friend moved to another state. Or crowd. Write about the losses in your journal.

Journals are not just for our sorrows, but for secrets, triumphs and joys.

Write about those too.

KEEP ON JOTTING

Write down memories, overheard conversations, obsessions, thoughts and reactions to what you see, read, hear, smell, touch and taste. Write down whatever else jogs your mind, stirs your emotions or gets you charged up.

It can be a word, a phrase, a thought that keeps entering your consciousness. It can be murderous, dark and recurring.

It can be anything you want.

Students often ask if they should do their "jotting" in the same journal as their long and often deeper entries or as Harriet the Spy does in a separate journal they carry around from work to the gym to home.

It doesn't matter.

Your entry may be a springboard for a finished piece. That has happened to me. My *Times* piece called "A New Mother's Confessions of Ambivalence" began as random jottings. I began it in the middle of the night when I was giving my daughter a bottle. The ideas poured out. I kept coming back. A floodgate had been opened.

Notice if your journal entries stay with you. Or haunt you. Or trigger something further you wish to say. It might indicate you're on the trail of something larger. Something hot.

Exercise

1 Buy a journal if you don't already have one.

2 Write your first (or next) entry on how you feel about keeping a journal or about what I told you about mine.

3 On a regular basis, start writing what you want in it. Try to spend twenty minutes a day.

CHAPTER TWENTY-THREE

My Mother and Willy Loman

Great things are done when men and mountains meet; This is not done by jostling in the street.

—*William Blake*

Before ever I read or saw *Death of a Salesman*, my mother was fond of telling me about a particular scene. It is the one in which Willy Loman is in the reception area of his neighbor Charley's office waiting for him to come out. Charley's son, Bernard, is there too. He is on his way to Washington, DC, and stopped in to see his dad. He and Willy talk for a while. Bring their personal histories to date.

Charley emerges. He sends Bernard off with his very best wishes, then turns to Willy and says, "Is that something? He's trying a case before the Supreme Court."

"The Supreme Court!" Willy, of course, is incredulous. He and Bernard had been talking so much about themselves. How come he's just hearing this now? "He didn't tell me."

Then Charley says those famous words, the ones I was told to take in: "He didn't have to. He's going to do it."

Didn't talk about it. Gonna do it.

Truly life's great divide.

Those who work and accomplish don't yap. And those who yap don't do.

Talk about writers telling the truth. Talk about mother's nourishment. I could forgive the canned and Bird's Eye vegetables. She fed me nurturing lines.

It wasn't that Miller's lines got me crackin'. I'd been secretly writing for years. What hearing that truth—and from my mother yet—did was show me what blowhards and dreamers and whiners were about, and remind me to shut my own trap.

And quietly take care of business whatever my business was.

JUST DO IT

Those who want to write—and not dream or talk—best sit there and get the words down.

I know many people who want to write. I know more who want to be writers. The former work hard and keep at it. And at it.

The latter mostly talk.

I had a student—I'll call her Joyce—who took my class to be a writer. She bought the books I recommended and required. She bought seven others too. Each week she brought in a new one she had discovered and devoured.

A must-read she told the others.

She also brought in flyers for writing conferences and readings she attended or planned to attend when she wasn't reading the books. Just being around editors and "other writers" was so exciting and enriching she was charged up to go to more.

"When do you find time to write?" another student asked her. Write?

The books and conferences and lectures and talks kept her away from her desk.

And self.

She said she hoped to get to it soon. At the moment she had to put all her belongings in cartons. She was getting ready to move. Again. In the last three years, she had moved four times. It had become a way of life.

"Write about moving," I said.

She started a piece, working on it a few afternoons a week at a Barnes & Noble cafe over lattés and café au laits.

"I really love to watch the people. I hate being alone in a room," she said.

Not music to a writing teacher's ears, but OK, alone isn't always comfy.

"Let's see what you've written," I said.

She brought in two pages about moving. It had merit. Everyone agreed. We gave her suggestions for fleshing the piece out more fully. I let my students take the lead. Everyone wanted more.

"More what?" I asked.

"More of why the author is really moving and from what she is running away," someone said.

Joyce nodded. I hoped she was taking it in. And for all I know she did. Perhaps that was why she left that night and never came to class again.

I get to know my students and what they can and cannot hear. Some listen and are open. They revise and improve. Then there are those who think it is cool to be a writer. Joyce is on that team.

I have had many Joyces in my classes who don't write, but do writer things.

There is another kind of salesman/writer. My student Mac was one. His work was engaging. His voice was appealing. I told him right away.

I let him know, too, how he could make his work stronger and quite possibly publishable. He put time and energy into revising.

But more into changing his fonts.

His next submission was in boldface. He had two-inch titles

leaping out. The one after that was in script. Sometimes he would have huge bold titles *and* script leads and the rest of the piece in caps.

His showiness was only part of it. He wrote titillating leads. More often than not, they were more shocking than artful. His sales pitch began to wear thin.

"Your words are speaking just fine for themselves," I told him. "I think you can simmer down."

Mac simmered a bit and wrote some more, but was still intent on strutting his stuff. Every paragraph had a curse word or a sexual innuendo.

On the top of his manuscript, I wrote that he needn't show off and try to dazzle.

Except he wanted to dazzle.

Mac isn't taking my class anymore. Or writing or revising. He's putting his material together and becoming a performance artist.

The job of a writer is to communicate, not sell. To pare it down to the truth. Or, as my friend, a fashion designer, is fond of saying, "Just wear the little black dress."

Advice

Think about some wisdom or a truth your mother or another adult imparted that once seemed irrelevant or even lame but has since turned into gold. Think of the context in which it was said. Think of what it has come to mean and how you have or have not used it.

Exercise

Write about it.

CHAPTER TWENTY-FOUR

George and Abe

The art of writing is the art of applying the seat of the pants to the seat of the chair.

—*Mary Heaton Vorse*

wo published writers were guests together at my class. I will call them George and Abe. Both follow their passions and write what they want, but in dramatically different ways. How they work and who they are was such an inspiration that I had them back the next semester and the next. They now have a regular gig.

Abe writes from the inside out. He begins with his feelings and experiences. After writing essays, stories and picture books, he has turned his hand to novels. A recently published story tells what happens to a long-term friendship when one friend is HIV-positive. The novel he is now writing is about a gay male coming of age.

"I write to make sense of the world and my place in it," Abe told my class. "I write to figure things out."

George, on the other hand, turns his interests, hobbies and fascinations into books for all ages. He learns everything he can about his passions through research and personal experiences and then writes about them with different slants and from every conceivable angle. He has done books on politics, history, cars, basketball, baseball and numerous other sports, becoming a maven on the topics he loves and making them His Own.

George writes about his outside passions as Abe does his inner life: with his entire being regularly present and a total commitment to the process. Yet their processes, habits and routines are as different as what turns them on.

I have known Abe now for many years and have watched his work unfold. It is increasingly self-revelatory. And far more deeply felt. With a full-time day job he is not about to quit, he writes on weekends and late at night.

George never works in the evening. He is in bed most nights by nine. Then up each morning at five and at his writing desk by 5:30. For six days a week that's his normal schedule. When he is in the throes of a book, he works seven. He doesn't write in the afternoons. He does his busy work then. That involves going to the library, making calls, conducting interviews or making notes for his next project. George works on several books at a time, each at different stages. There is the one he is writing, the one he is researching and the one he is starting to explore.

Unlike Abe, who is clueless about what will come out before he sits down at his desk, George knows before he stops each day what he will write the next.

No secrets. No magic. They both write what is in their hearts. And regularly.

One works around a nine-to-five job and from the center of his gut. The other shows up each day before dawn to explore his outside passions. Different kinds of writers with different routines, yet like Arthur Miller's Bernard, who's trying a case before the Supreme Court, both are quietly *doing it*.

Exercise

1 Describe your writing schedule and approach. Are you more like George or Abe? Which feels the most and least comfortable? With which do you feel you are most yourself? Why?

2 List three topics you are dying to write about. Circle the one that leaps out at you. Begin to write about it. Stay with it for forty minutes. Make notes on how to carry on.

CHAPTER TWENTY-FIVE

If You Ask People How They Are, They Might Tell You

*I don't know about bores. Maybe you shouldn't feel so sorry
if you see some swell girl married to them. They don't hurt
anybody, most of them, and maybe they're all terrific whistlers
or something.*

—Holden Caulfield

The impulse to express ourselves is profound.

You know this because you want to do it. Right? And you are sitting here now reading a book that will help you find that way.

You know this, too, if you have been in the company of lawyers. Or have lived through too many dates.

And you certainly know from asking people how they are, because far too often they tell you. They tell you how they are. And were. And about each member of their families. They tell you who's got kidney stones, who lost his job, and how everyone's medication is working.

They go on and on and on. Mentally you've already bid them adieu.

Colossal windbags make us twitch and squirm. They don't relate to us or to themselves. Or to anyone on this planet.

When my daughter was in nursery school, we got a lift every morning with a neighbor whose son was a classmate. Monday through Friday I listened to this mother for the entire ride. Her random thoughts had nothing to do with our kids, their school or with me, but I sat in the front "uh-huhing" her week after nauseating week.

Until her track-lighting speech.

I didn't have track lighting. I wasn't in the market. And I never indicated in any way that it was one of my favorite topics. One morning, though, this woman spent fifteen solid minutes giving me the prices, measurements and installation charges of every track light in every store in New York from the Bowery to The Bronx.

There is no such thing as a free lunch or free rides. After that I decided we'd walk.

As writers, you don't want to bore readers. You want to keep them in the tent. So unless it's germane to your story or your point, spare them what you went through shopping for track lighting.

How do you make a connection with readers and keep them fully engaged?

By connecting with what is inside of you and being fully engaged yourself. This means picking subjects you care about deeply.

And having something to say.

"How do you decide what to write about?" people ask me.

I look at the things in my life that obsess me, that play over and over in my heart and mind.

The things I write about matter to me. They matter to me a

lot. They haunt and nudge and delight and rage me. The passion must be strong.

Write about what matters to you. Examine your psyches, memories and worlds. Look inward. Pull it out. Write where your energy is. From where you are most alive. It's what Pat Conroy calls "the center of the storm."

Advice

1 To become more conscious of who and what engages you and who and what puts you off, pay attention when you ask people how they are. Physically or mentally take notes.

2 When you are asked the same question, what do you say? Observe others' reactions. Are they interested? Wanting more? Or less?

3 Give some thought about what you gravitate and respond to in others and what others respond to in you. Think about what is likable and what is not.

The same is true with your writing.

4 Think about people who are egocentric and those who have touched your soul. What can you learn from each that you can use in your writing?

Exercise

Write about something in your life that turned out differently from what you expected. It can be anything from a meatloaf to a marriage. Take out information, details and anything else that you wouldn't want to hear.

CHAPTER TWENTY-SIX

The Subtext

*I often think that a slightly exposed shoulder emerging from
a long satin nightgown packed more sex than two naked
bodies in bed.*

—*Bette Davis*

O ne evening on my way to class, I ran into another writing instructor. She had just sold an essay to the Sunday *Times* Hers column. The title was "Fear of Dying." I asked her what it was about.

"On the surface, it's about how I started dying my hair, but it's *really* about my fear of becoming my mother."

What came to mind immediately was Mel Brooks's two-thousand-year-old man's line: "We mock the things we are to be."

My friend's underlying theme.

I thought about my own Hers piece. If someone asked what "My Mostly Companion" was about, what would be my answer?

It's about two experiences I had with my daughter: bathing suit shopping and bumping into an old beau, but it's *really* about the complexity of our relationship and how my daughter is not always the child, but sometimes a sister, mother and friend.

I started thinking about my other pieces—the ones that worked and didn't. The ones that did could be summed up in my writer friend's two-part sentence:

On the surface it's about blah, blah, blah, but it's *really* about blah, blah.

My misses have a first part only. There isn't any "but it's *really*."

"The Grandfather Connection" is about my daughter and father swimming laps together, but it's *really* about love without expectations. The kind grandparents give.

"On Not Looking Like Catherine Deneuve" is about what I've gone through not being a chiseled beauty, but it's *really* about having to work harder and take more chances when you don't have it, which, in the long run, is better news.

There must be a subtext to your work. What is it *really about*? What's happening between the lines?

My student Carla's essay "My Lover Committed Suicide" is about what she went through when her college boyfriend killed himself, but it is *really* about how we are each responsible for our own lives and that no matter how much we love another human being, we cannot prevent certain things.

My student Michele's "Hunting for a New Therapist" is about shopping for a new shrink, but it is *really* about how hard it is to find people with whom we can connect.

Her other *Times* piece, "They Don't Take Just Any Mutt," is about getting her golden retrievers admitted to a dog run, but it is *really* about the chase being more fun than the arrival.

SUBTEXT—WITH AND WITHOUT

I had a student—I'll call him Joe—who came to New York to act. When that didn't happen the way he had dreamed, he started cleaning apartments for men.

He vacuumed.

He dusted.

He Pledged.

He did more.

The "more" was what brought Joe to my class. In addition to cleaning, Joe got naked and serviced his clients in a "for men only" way.

My home is downtown Manhattan. My neighborhood is quite gay. I have traveled far since I watched *What's My Line?* in the fifties. Yet Joe's story got me good.

Why?

The subtext.

On the surface Joe's piece was about his experiences as a gay male prostitute, but it was *really* about the prostitute part in every person and the price one pays to survive.

Every student in my class was totally blown away.

That same semester I had another student—I will call her Jane—who also wrote about sex. Unlike Joe, she was heterosexual and did not do it for cash. Jane wrote about what went on in her bedroom with her last two sexual partners.

The piece did not work. Jane made me squirm. I wanted out of her bedroom. Fast.

"But didn't you squirm watching Joe?" she asked.

"More," I told her, "but so did he."

Joe, as the writer, stepped back and watched his own actions. He had a definite point of view. He was humiliated and anguished in his sexual exploits. His self-loathing clearly came through. In telling me so much about his life he told me truths about mine.

Jane did not get under her own skin. Or give me anything to chew on. Telling about her exploits in bed was exhibitionistic, but hardly revealing. She did not share who she was in her bedroom or how she felt about the encounters. I felt as if she were posturing.

Elizabeth Crow, editor in chief of *Mademoiselle*, says that what she looks for in personal essays is the writer's inward journey.

"We read to learn truths about ourselves and our lives," Crow said.

As a writer, you must deliver them.

You don't have to know what your pieces are about at the onset. You needn't know midway. But at some point at the end of a draft or a few, you should make discoveries, surprise yourself and see what is propelling you through.

The "what it is *really* about" or subtext comes from the center of your gut. If it is not what is fueling you forward, take a closer look.

Joe's deeply felt piece made me look at myself and the things I do to survive. Through his encounters, he revealed who he is and who the reader is too. It was there between the lines.

In commenting on Jane's work, another student told her, "We don't have a clue how you feel about sex. Or the guys. Or yourself."

Physically Jane was naked. Emotionally she hid.

Exercise

Go back and look at the pieces you have written. What are they about on the surface?

What are they *really* about?

Rework the ones that seem to be missing the subtext. Uncover your "ahas."

CHAPTER TWENTY-SEVEN

The Difference Between "Aha" and "Oy Vay"

The liberty of the individual must be thus far limited; he must not make himself a nuisance to other people.

—*John Stuart Mill*

M y minister student, whom I discussed in an earlier chapter, was critiquing another student's essay. The piece did not work. Everyone agreed, but no one could figure out why. According to the reverend, it was missing that big "Aha."

Spoken, I thought, like a man of the cloth who majored and minored in sermons. I thought it over carefully. My minister was right.

Good writing requires disclosure. It is self-revelatory and arrives at a basic "aha." That involves looking at your experiences and seeing the truths—both the dark and the light—so you can *share* them with readers who will nod and say, "Yes, that is how it is. You are speaking to me. I have been there too."

That is different from self-absorption, which is a preoccupation with one's self and is not about sharing at all. It is kvetching on paper. It's annoying and ungiving. Readers will be turned off.

When you write, you want to reveal something about yourself and your experiences that illuminates your readers' lives. You are taking them on your journey to see the discoveries you have made delivering the truths they subconsciously know. Offering fresh insights on who they are and where they fit in.

Giving thoughts to chew on between the lines.

Something that will surprise.

You don't want readers to finish reading and ask, "What was this about?"

Or worse, "Why did I waste my time?"

Self-revelation is a gift to both writer and reader. Self-absorption is anything but. There must be a payoff for trailing us through the experience. Something should become clear.

The difference between self-revelation and self-absorption is the difference between "aha" and "oy vay."

Between a nod of recognition and "so what?"

"So what?" was a writing buddy's hard-hitting comment when several essays of mine missed the mark. He said that about more than one. The "so whatest" piece I ever wrote was about my experiences being short, beginning in the second grade when we had to line up according to height. Joan Factor was the only person shorter than I was. She was also absent a lot with bad colds. "Please send her to school," I said to God every morning, "with or without the phlegm."

That was the "cutest" part of my "being short" essay. From my prayers, it got even worse. It was missing the components of a good personal experience piece: the arrival at a truth, a point of view and emotional involvement.

It was definitely missing "me."

Like my student Jane who wrote about sex, I didn't impart wisdom or offer any "ahas." The piece was flat. It sounded cataloguish. Like the résumé of a short person.

That was not true of Garry Trudeau's essay "My Inner Shrimp." The opening sentence was arresting, "For the rest of my days, I shall be a recovering short person."

The rest of the piece was as good.

It went somewhere. It was about something. The truth he arrived at is most people's truth—whether we are vertically challenged or not—no matter who we are or what we become as adults, we perceive ourselves the way we and our peers did when we were growing up.

If you go deeply enough into your own soul, you articulate what people feel.

Once a shrimp, always a shrimp. It warmed my heart to read that. Trudeau's words hit the right notes.

For a few minutes, I felt tall.

Exercise

Write about a physical trait you had while growing up that you wished was different or caused you distress. Capture what you went through using one or more scenes and show the "aha" at which you arrive.

CHAPTER TWENTY-EIGHT

Likable Voices

A pen may or may not be mightier than the sword, but it is brassier than the telephone. When the writer converses privately with her soul in the long dark night, a thousand neighbors are listening in on the party line, taking it personally.

—Barbara Kingsolver

I recently told a new friend over dinner how thrilled I am when someone compliments my voice. My dinner companion's response was, "I didn't know you could sing."

I can't. And don't. Except to accompany myself at the piano when no one is around.

But my voice—my writing voice—I have been cultivating that for years.

And if you have been doing the exercises here, you've been cultivating your voice too.

Our voices are how we see and say it.

It is our way of putting it into words.

The sound of ourselves on paper.

It is who we are on the page.

It is a lifelong process paring it down and sounding like ourselves on that page. It takes time. Going inward.

And writing. And writing. And writing.

In the examples of my work in previous sections, I shared different parts of myself. Me as an eight-year-old younger sister being pushed away. Me as a mother alone. Me before a three-way mirror looking at less-than-perfect thighs.

Ouch!

Telling the truth about our lives is no walk in the park. It takes a willingness to be open. It requires showing who we are.

With my own work, my students' or whomever I am reading, the words and feelings must ring true.

The examples I gave in earlier sections from Russell Baker's memoirs certainly have that ring. He knows his mother's voice so well he can artfully bring it right to us.

In *Operating Instructions* and in *Bird by Bird*, Anne Lamott sounds as if she is right there in her pajamas at the slumber party. She is vulnerable. Honest. And always, always real.

That's the kind of writing I love. It is like the voice of a friend on the phone. Totally there. Totally authentic. Honest. Likable. Sincere.

Remember our discussion earlier about being with colossal bores? It's a drag and a half. You want to be anywhere but there.

It can be the person bores you. Or whines.

Or has nothing interesting or relevant to say.

Or doesn't connect to the words coming out.

And cannot connect to you.

It's the same deal on the paper.

Readers can't spend time with a writer whose voice they do not like.

BE SINCERE

I have a student whom I will call Ruth. She recently left her husband. She has started writing about it. What she brings to class sounds like a cross between an infomercial and Helen Reddy's "I Am Woman."

As much as Ruth wanted out of the marriage and despite her ex being a certifiable "louse," she wasn't honest discussing the breakup. She failed to mention the hurt.

The class did not buy Ruth's "I'm cool without him" refrain. I told her time would help. Time and distance to gain some perspective. To own up to the truth.

Readers identify with honesty. No one has it all figured out.

A good writer struggles with the big and small questions, then looks within to sort things out.

Sincerity is the touchstone of a likable voice. Readers want to be touched. If you aren't going to tell the Truth about your life, do something—anything—other than write.

In Manhattan it is easy to want to sound politically correct. For raising children, instilling values and living morally, Political Correctness is splendid. For having a voice that is honest and real, Political Correctness stinks.

It is back to self-revelation. To connecting to your true self.

Don't posture.

Don't lie.

Don't perform.

Be yourself. Be sincere. Tell the truth about your life.

Exercise

Write about another experience from your childhood that changed your life. Tell the truth.

CHAPTER TWENTY-NINE

Oona the Tuna and Onward

He didn't start out like that. He just kept doing it and doing it and doing it and doing it. That's why now it sings.

—*A student explaining the writerly growth of Oona's creator*

*I*t was Lou's last evening in my Wednesday night workshop. He'd been my student for over five years. He brought in the last chapter of his second novel, which he began to read. Then for the first time since he had been in my class, he stopped. His voice started to quiver. I was on his right. He turned to me and very quietly said, "Could you finish?"

I got through a paragraph, but the words got stuck. I turned to Jill on my other side and asked, "Would you?"

She did. Clearly and forcefully. When she finished the last chapter, I reached over and hugged Lou. It was a wonderful end to a wonderful book. Several members of the group had been there since chapter one.

Hanna, another longtime student, was sitting there quietly

repeating, "Oh my god," and "I can't believe it," and "You did it again."

Hanna and I then reminisced about the night Lou brought in the final chapter of his last book. A snowstorm had hit that day. Five of the seven students in the group were absent. It had been Hanna, Lou and me.

Lou's last chapter of that first book needed work. Hanna and I told him.

He wrote it, made it stronger and revised the entire book. It was published. Lou returned to the workshop to write a second. It's an even deeper, more heartfelt book.

DIALOGUE

Lou appeared in my class and my life when he took my course "Writing for Children." I saw something there early on and clearly let him know.

His writing touched me—there was feeling there—and Lou definitely wanted to write. He gave it his all. That was immediately apparent. He showed up with manuscripts, was open to criticism, revised and revised some more.

He was as eager to give help as he was to get it, offering others constructive criticism, adding much to the class discussions.

Lou is an attorney. A litigator yet. Stumbling on one who wore his feelings on the sleeves of his gray suits gave me reason to rejoice. I figured if I did nothing else in my life that amounted to much, turning one litigator into a writer of sensitive stories would be plenty.

As terrific a student as Lou had been, he had two areas that needed work. I hounded him about one every week. I never mentioned the other.

The first, the most common problem I know of as both a teacher and a practitioner, is *overwriting*.

Lou explained things fine, and also in more than one way. As he became a better writer, he learned how to tighten and cut.

When you pare it down, say it once or less (remember some things are better left unsaid), you'll keep readers more involved than if you lecture them or nag.

If you had or are a mother, you know precisely what I mean.

Lou's weakest area with overwriting—and this may be yours too—was in dialogue. He first explained how someone would say something. Then he'd have the person's actual words. Then for those who hadn't caught on yet, he'd sum up what the person said.

We attributed this to Lou's being a lawyer and given to summations. When we were done "attributing" we eliminated the befores and afters and just had the character speak.

Don't explain what is going to be or has already been said. Your dialogue itself should say it. If it doesn't, rewrite it. Something's wrong.

Now with the dialogue itself: Lou did something else initially that may also apply to you. He had people talk in full sentences, not having yet developed an "ear."

For example, he'd write, "Do you want to come over?" until he realized that people don't speak in full sentences.

"Want to come over?" was better. "Come over?" better still.

If you have too many full sentences, cut them back.

And rather than having a ho-hum answer to the above like, "Sure I'd love to" or "I can't" or "I can't because I'm going to my grandmother's," it's better to have a response that shows tension, illuminates the character or situation, or moves the story along. Something like:

"We always play at your house" or "I can't. I'm going to Mary's" or "Can I stay for dinner too? My mother's going to the hospital again" would be more compelling.

Note how the above shows conflict, layers the character and puts a new twist in the plot.

Lou's other area that needed work—the one I chose to ignore—was his propensity for cuteness. In his early stories, he tagged on morals at the end in case the reader was too stupid to get it. He also had a tendency to sound like Mary Poppins. Occasionally he'd have a phrase or title that was more than a wee bit cloying.

One was *Oona the Tuna.*

He sent *Oona the Tuna* to publishers. I never said a word. The story itself was lovely. I assumed that if it was accepted the editors would have him change the title. And should they like it, the world would have a tuna by the name of Oona.

It didn't sell. We were disappointed. I shared my thoughts about his title and why I hadn't told him earlier: He had bigger fish to fry.

Lou is revising his second novel now. It's strong. And touching and real. The most immediate parts—the ones that sing—are written in dialogue.

Here are five lessons to learn from Lou's dialogue and tuna:

1. You can really go far if you want to write.
2. You can go even further if you revise.
3. Virtually everyone has to pare it down.
4. Virtually everyone finds some aspects of writing hard.
5. Even litigators feel.

Advice

Listen to people in restaurants, on buses, at work and wherever you are. Listen to people you know and to your own conversations.

Exercise

1 Write down a conversation you've overheard or the gist of it. Make up a scene around it using it as a center.

2 Have a pad, a file in your computer or a section of a notebook where you can jot down titles. Write them there whenever they come to you.

CHAPTER THIRTY

Lousy First Drafts

To fall in love with a first draft to the point where one cannot change it is to greatly enhance the prospects of never publishing.

—*Richard North Patterson*

*I*n the beginning was The Word. After that comes lousy first drafts. *The Sun Also Rises* didn't just rise. It rose and set many times.

I didn't always know this. I thought I was the only one. The only one whose first drafts were clunky while every real writer's were gems. I assumed they just sat down and wrote masterpieces like I once assumed Gene Kelly just danced.

Then I began to see the light. The rehearsal halls. The sweat. It is about letting go, losing self-consciousness and putting down words, without thinking about anything, especially the result.

When author Judy Blume was a guest at my class, she told my students she never sent her editor anything before a fifth draft. The first four are between her and her.

Philip Roth wrote and discarded more than 180 pages before he got his opening paragraph of his memoir *Patrimony*. Ann Beattie showed her manuscript of *Chilly Scenes of Winter* to a friend, "and he returned it with the bottom part of page 59 renumbered page 1. He'd thrown the rest away. So page 60 became page 2, etc. It's OK for the writer to feel his or her way into the material, but the reader doesn't have to suffer through it." (Excerpted from *Writer's Digest* magazine.)

Barbara Kingsolver wrote: "I always have to write at least a hundred pages that go into the trash can before it finally begins to work. . . . I try to consider them pages 100 to 0. . . ." (p. 25, *The Basics of Writing Bestsellers*, vol. 17.)

Lousy first drafts and false starts are the deal with the greats. And with every writer I know. Their published work is not their first burst. It is umpteen drafts beyond.

I could spend the rest of this book giving you examples with more quotes from the greats. Instead let's discuss how you can go about writing lousy drafts too.

Advice

Start by giving yourself the assignment to write something terrible. I mean it. Begin something. And go on. And on. Don't try to smooth it. Or polish it. Or make it sing. Just let the words come out of you.

Remember those people in your life who belittled you, expected perfection or criticized your every move? They are not looking over your shoulder now and will not enter your room. If you feel your internal naysayers are about to charge in, send them on sabbatical this minute or even to the moon. No one is going to see what you're writing. Not your mother. Your ex. Or your kids. First drafts are between you and you.

Suspend judgment. Forget perfection. Pretend you are boogying alone in a room. Get the words out. Keep them coming. Expect a big amorphous mess.

Then from this unwieldy, lousy first draft, begin to shape and structure and form. As Alexander Portnoy's therapist said, "So. Now ve may perhaps to begin."

"Don't be afraid to discard work you know isn't up to standard. Don't try to save junk just because it took you a long time to write it," wrote David Eddings (*The Basics of Writing Bestsellers*, p. 25).

Get it down. Don't stop after every two sentences to read what you've written. Or second-guess yourself. Just get an entire draft done. It doesn't matter how it sounds or how many things are wrong. There's something there in the cluttered mess. You'll discover it as you chisel it down.

"You have to waste tons and tons of paper if you are going to be a writer. . . . Good writing stems from mistakes." (Anne Lamott, *Writer's Digest*, June 1996, p. 32.)

Exercise

Freewrite. Just turn on your computer or take a blank piece of paper and write about something you have been thinking of for a while. Allow it to just come up. Allow it to be less than a jewel.

CHAPTER THIRTY-ONE

Night Came: Six Tips for Tightening

Be careful that you write accurately rather than much.
—Desiderius Erasmus

Winston Churchill once sent someone a very long letter and at the end was the following postscript:

I would have made it shorter, but I didn't have the time.

You do, though. Unlike Churchill, you have time and are alive. Very alive. Probably more alive than you have ever been if you are writing regularly. That is one of the joys of writing. It wakes you up to both the outside and your inner worlds and makes you more conscious and alive.

Yet as conscious and alive as writers are, there is often resistance to revision.

Why?

Partly because of the mistaken notion that our first bursts

should sound like Raymond Carver at his best. Also we tend to fall in love with our every word. This attachment can make it hard to let go.

What parts can we possibly delete? How much? How little? And why? Cutting words that come from the self can feel like amputation.

Revising becomes easier the longer we write and the more we engage in the process. Then we see how pruning and tightening can make our writing sing.

Nora Ephron says, "In the course of writing a short essay— 1500 words, that's only six double-spaced pages—I often used 300 to 400 pieces of typing paper. . . ." (*New Woman*, November 1991, p. 51.)

Here are six suggestions to help you start wasting paper too:

Take a class. I will devote several later sections to what you should look for and can expect from writing classes, but for the moment I want to say that a good teacher and class can be invaluable for revisions. It is often too hard to see how to revise one's own work. We all need others' eyes.

Let your draft sit a while. Put your first draft away for a while before beginning the next. Do the same with your successive ones too. Creating this distance cools you off and gives you a better perspective. You will view your work more objectively when you are not sitting right on top of it.

Without distance, revisions are often Band-Aids. And not even the regular size, but the kind that don't even cover the smallest boo-boos: those little junior strips.

That is not to say you should avoid making changes when something good, something brilliant strikes. Quite often when I am in the throes of a project, I wake up in the middle of the night or at dawn with ideas, sentences and better ways to say it. I don't close my eyes and hold out for perspective. If something "gets me" I write it down.

Read your work aloud. Do this in classes. Do it alone. If it sounds clunky and wordy, it is.

Tighten beginnings. Years ago I wrote a series of four children's books for one publisher. I submitted a book at a time. My editor called when she received my first. I asked for her opinion.

"It's on my desk. I haven't yet read it, but I can probably tell you what I tell most authors; the first two chapters can go."

I did not eventually cut the entire two chapters, but, yes, I eliminated enormous chunks.

When my students hand in, say, a five-page piece, I can often— without even reading it—point to the bottom of the first page or the middle of the second and say, "Your piece could start right here."

Beginnings are often foreplay. They warm the writer up to the material, help her work her way in. Readers aren't required to see this work.

Beginning chunks can often go.

Don't talk to your readers like they have been left back. Television has something to do with it. So does a lack of trust in the reader. Writers overexplain and repeat themselves for fear the reader is a passive lump.

I majored in overwriting. I can be a nagging mother in print. Of course, I don't see it in my first drafts so I say it again.

And again.

And again.

With humor, overwriting is a killer. Brevity truly counts. Too many words make it sink right there on the page.

In my *Times* travel piece on the Fire Island beachhouse, which I discussed in a previous section, I felt as if my editor eliminated more then he left in.

For example, I had a running thing about espadrilles and another on getting clams. He cut two times I discussed the "espadrilles" and two expeditions for clams.

"But I thought those were the funniest parts of the piece," I said.

"They are," he said. "When you use them once."

When it comes to funny—I mean really funny—I always think of Jack Benny. He got laughs by saying nothing.

Condense. You don't need every moment in every scene. Or every person. Or every word said.

You want emotional honesty, not necessarily the literal truth. Omit whatever and whomever doesn't enhance your story, slows it down or clutters it up.

A student of mine wrote a touching, funny essay about a car trip with her family. In early drafts, she included every day, every evening and every stop. Each draft got smoother. And closer to the mark.

One particular evening on her trip added nothing to the story. Compared to other moments, the events were rather mundane. Yet my student devoted a page and a half to what did and didn't happen that night. Everyone kept telling her sentences and words to cut.

I didn't think that would do it. I told her, "Take out the entire scene."

"Then what do I put in its place?" she asked.

"How about 'Night came'?"

She took out the scene, put in "Night came" then got to what happened the next day.

It worked. It flowed. That scene wasn't necessary. Without it, the piece was a gem.

Sometimes all you need is a two-word sentence: Night came.

Exercise

Go back to your early drafts of the exercises you've done and revise them using the above techniques.

CHAPTER THIRTY-TWO

Not Enough Cocktail Lounge: Nine More Tips for Revising

I would sometimes bring in my first draft to show my students.
I would tell them: "You have to have a longing to make it
good. If you don't have that longing, you're not a writer."
—Grace Paley

Getting rid of excesses is a big part of revising. Other things improve your work too. Here are nine more suggestions:

Don't exercise your literary muscles. My father, a voracious reader and a lover of big words, surprised me when upon finishing *Lonesome Dove*, a book he could not put down, said, "Best part was there were no fancy words. I breezed through it without having to look any up."

Before I was conscious of heart and soul, I thought big words were key. I'd get nowhere quickly as a writer with my pathetic vocabulary. As a reader, then a teacher, I felt intellectually impaired. "You say it well," I have told more than one student whose command of the language impressed me, never admitting I hadn't the foggiest just what it was they said.

Good writing, of course, is graceful and smooth. Using words effectively counts. But words should bring readers into a scene, not have them stand back in awe.

If you know big words and they organically work, don't consciously avoid them. But don't use them just to show off. You want to touch and involve readers with what you are saying, not dazzle or impress them.

Don't show off either with convoluted sentences or esoteric ideas. Be accessible. Straightforward. And sincere.

Don't pack in information. Reference books do that.

Be specific. Share your experience as colorfully as you can using specific, personal details. It has been decades since I read *The Sun Also Rises* yet I still see the corners of Brett Ashley's eyes crinkle as she spoke. In *The Prince of Tides* every place—New York, Charleston, Sullivan Island and the rest—is evoked in vivid details. Conroy describes each locale so well. And I can still hear Tom Wingo's voice no matter to whom he was speaking. And always I will hear and feel those last words he whispered: "Lowenstein. Lowenstein."

Avoid the abstract. Abstractions make work flat and generic. They don't invite readers into your world. Make them use their senses; they will more readily go on your journey. Poached salmon is better than fish. A black-watch kilt and navy turtleneck are better than a skirt and sweater. "Rhapsody in Blue" is better than a song. Better than any song.

Vary your sentences. Don't have one long sentence after another. Or too many short ones in a row. Intersperse short with long.

Vary the structure. Don't begin one sentence after the other with the same word. Especially if that word is "I."

Avoid clichés and overworked words. Don't say it the way most people would. Be fresh. Come up with your own ways of comparing and describing. Ways that are yours. And unique. Don't call your family "dysfunctional." Or use psychobabble, New Age lingo and self-help jargon. Everyone has beaten you to it. If someone is nuts, don't make him "mad as a hatter."

If someone is happy or on drugs, don't say she is as "high as a kite on the Fourth of July."

Speaking of the Fourth, find another cliché than fireworks to describe an orgasm.

Be scenic. Avoid telling. Don't explain that your big brother was a bully. Show him sitting on some puny runt's head. Don't say your teenager is surly. Have her snarl or tell you to "Chill."

It's back again to "show, don't tell." Dramatize whatever you can. No one wants to be told what's what. It's ho-hum. A sleeping pill.

Use dialogue. Don't tell us what you or someone else said. Let us hear it. As a reader I am pulled in by voices. I still hear Nora Ephron's mother in "A Few Words About Breasts" respond to Nora's desire for a bra with "What for?" And I am still haunted by the doctor in the first scene of *The Liar's Club* saying, "Show me the marks," to the young Mary Karr.

Deepen. Deepening requires more than what I can say in the next several sentences in a revision section. It requires a certain way of looking and viewing the world. With wisdom. Humanity. Openness. Self-reflection. Honesty.

Deepening means cutting through the pretension. It's about being real.

Having said that, I can now remind you to stop or pause throughout your work to ruminate, ponder, reflect and offer insights about the experience you are putting on the page.

In her essay, "I Don't Like That Nightgown," Anna Quindlen

writes about the security of knowing a spouse's reaction at any given time.

I put a plate of radicchio salad on the table, step back, and count to five. "What is this stuff?" my husband says suspiciously, poking it with his fork. It warms my heart.

And mine.

Don't fizzle at the ending. Telling you not to fizzle out is like telling you to deepen. It's really far more complicated and extensive than what a short space will allow.

Remember, though, that with endings, you should arrive at a truth. At that "aha." Why you trailed us through the experience. Your reason for writing the piece.

The reader is entitled to a payoff for hanging in. A smile. A tear. Or a chill.

Give her something to chew on. To contemplate.

A pow!

Strive to achieve a balance. I had a student who brought in a piece that began with a scene in a cocktail lounge. The group consensus was that the scene was too long. We suggested she tighten it.

The following week she brought in a new draft. It was missing the juice of the first. One of the reasons, we realized, was that she had taken out most of the cocktail lounge scene. We strongly suggested she put back some of the conversation and description.

"Too much cocktail lounge, not enough cocktail lounge," the student said. She sat there pulling on her hair.

That cocktail lounge phrase became the password of my Wednesday Night Workshop. We chanted it and laughed about it for many months to come.

The thing is this: You have to play. You have to try. Revising is hardly a science.

You have to take out parts of the cocktail lounge and put them back in again.

And it requires far more than two weeks and drafts to have your writing hang in balance.

When smoothing out an entire work, strive for mixing the various components. Combine description, scenes with dialogue and rumination.

The title of this book should really be "Revising From Personal Experience." That's what writing really is. Revising and revising and revising.

Exercise

Take a favorite piece of yours and revise it using the above nine tips.

CHAPTER THIRTY-THREE

Why You Hit Snags and What You Can Do

The trouble is all in the knob at the top of our bodies.

—Margaret Atwood

Did something happen to that sabbatical on which you sent your internal critics? Have they returned to bug you? Are they now breathing down your neck?

Or is something other than those naysayers keeping you from getting the words down?

Or to put it another way, is your resistance greater than your desire?

If you said "yes" to any or all of the above, you have plenty of company among writers from beginners to seasoned pros. Every writer knows what it means to be stuck. No one mounts the horse and just rides.

What are the impediments that writers face? How many of them apply to you?

The well is dry. If you have recently finished an assignment or essay, you may feel empty. Depleted. And totally spent. You have nothing more to say on the subject. Or about anything else.

How could you?

You've said it. And had it. What you need is space and time.

Marathon runners are drained and dehydrated when they cross the finish line. Six miles before that, they often hit something commonly known as "the wall."

It's similar for writers after we have been revealing what is inside. There is virtually nothing else to come out besides our internal organs.

Don't panic. Don't get deranged. Don't think you should fold up your tent.

You will have plenty to say again.

Writing takes great effort and energy. We pour it out and make something exist where nothing existed before. When we give ourselves completely to it, we come out totally spent.

This happens to me after every essay. And in a big-time way with books. My creative life is over. It's curtains. Or drapes. The end.

Then I get an idea. Recall an experience. Or something starts clicking in my mind. I'm taking notes. Putting words on napkins. And at it once again.

It takes a long time to understand this process.

Even longer to accept it.

If you have recently finished something, don't push. At least don't push right now. Take time to pause. Be still. Be quiet.

It will bubble up again.

There may be other reasons for not writing, though, besides an empty well. Before we discuss the remedies, let's see what they are about.

You demand perfection. You have noticed the words you are putting on your page or screen do not have quite the same ring as, say, Shakespeare's. Or are as polished as Somerset Maugham's. So you ask yourself, isn't it silly to torture myself when it comes out sounding like mush?

Why bother? What's the point?

Did you forget that no one's first bursts are perfectly formed? That sparkling prose doesn't just leap out? Carol Shields quietly wrote for decades before gaining critical acclaim. It took Elmore Leonard more than thirty years to become an overnight success.

Demanding perfection kills the joy and the process. It's the uptight adults on your back. Get rid of them and hang out with the child who enjoys playing in the sand.

Don't invite your internal critics back for Homecoming. Let them visit someone else.

The genre feels wrong. There is more than one way to express yourself. More than one way to make your voice heard. My student Lou wrote picture books until he found the right tone in novels.

I tried a whodunit. It just wasn't me. Neither were books for preschoolers.

A very good picture book editor helped point the way with feedback on a story I'd submitted. She said my humor and voice sounded more "adult" and suggested I turn it around.

I did. I told the story from the mother's voice. My own. In one essay. Then in another.

The first-person has been my primary form, but I am always trying new ones. The fat lady hasn't sung her song. She probably won't until I'm six feet under.

Try different forms and genres. See where you live and what feels most alive.

You hit on your truths and it's scary. *Mais oui.* Virtually all of my long-term students go through this. *Moi aussi.* From time to time.

So we crawl back into our shells. And hide from ourselves and the world as most people regularly do. Then we poke out and begin to say it again, because hiding is so much worse.

Just last week I ran into a writer who'd just finished a personal piece. Her regular gig is corporate reports. For the first time since her SATs, she's plagued with insomnia.

"I can't believe I am saying this stuff," she said.

I asked, "Was writing about budgets more fun?"

She smiled. "It's just that whoever reads it will know what I've been through."

"And fortunately now so do you."

No one forces us to put ourselves on paper. We want to more than we don't. Admittedly, it can be scary. Telling the truth is like sharing a secret. It is not "the good girl" way.

Accept that this fear might occasionally hit you. It's intermittently part of the deal. For now, poke your head out a smidgen. Inch by inch will do.

You haven't hit on anything. As scary as it can be seeing the truths pour out, it is even worse when they don't. You may be putting yourself to sleep. Or wondering why you are even bothering to put words down at all, because what you are saying is not connected to who you are. And sounds like total mush.

Going through the motions is deadening.

Not feeling what you are writing is a signal something's wrong.

Years ago, I wrote profiles, features and assorted "out there" pieces. One in particular was a struggle. It was a 750-word piece on double-decker buses, which I was doing for a New York neighborhood newspaper.

I couldn't come up with a lead.

At the time I was pregnant and filling up journals. In all my entries I said the same thing: I didn't want to write "out there" pieces with so much happening inside.

That was where I wanted to look. And where I eventually turned.

Pregnancy often signals us to look more deeply within.

Even if you aren't carrying a child, check what's happening inside. Here are twenty-two more suggestions for when you are stuck:

1. Give it a rest for a little while.
2. Take walks.
3. Exercise.
4. Read a book you've been meaning to read, newspapers, magazines and the work of an author you admire.
5. Reread a favorite book.
6. Go to movies, plays, the ballet, the opera and museums.
7. See friends.
8. Meditate.
9. Take a class.
10. Write in your journal.
11. Expand on something you hit on in your journal.
12. Continue with that.
13. Write an open letter.
14. Reread some of your old work.
15. Rewrite the last paragraph of whatever you were working on.
16. Carry on with that.
17. Or with something else that is germinating.
18. Change the place you write.
19. Change the way you write. Write longhand if you used a computer or vice versa.
20. Change the time you write.
21. Write shorter assignments.
22. Reward yourself after you've gotten it down.

CHAPTER THIRTY-FOUR

Is It Funny?

I remain just one thing, and one thing only—and that is a clown. It places me on a far higher plane than any politician.
—Charlie Chaplin

dmittedly, humor is subjective. We all laugh at different things. Is there a way then for writers to say it funny? Or funnier?

First let's look at what humor is.

REAL LIFE

I think the Number One Thing that makes people laugh is The Truth. The Truth with a curlycue at the end. It's a special way of looking at life. One that requires distance. Perspective. A sense of the ridiculous. Like Gilda Radner and Erma Bombeck clearly had.

Radner pointed out life's absurdities through Emily Litella, Roseanne Roseannadanna and her other memorable, idiosyncratic characters. She inhabited these kooky, invented people with their extreme yet lovable traits. Erma Bombeck told the truth about daily living by being one of us. She was herself, not a made-up character, right there on the page. Yet both looked at the human condition through brightly twinkling eyes.

According to Charlie Chaplin, life is a tragedy from the close shot and a comedy from the long shot. Seeing it funny takes standing back and looking through the long lens. It's the way Neil Simon views what living with another person is like in *The Odd Couple* and *Barefoot in the Park*. The truth he arrived at: It is downright hard. Look at what Felix and Oscar go through. Look at Corie's and Paul's first-first fights. The former were great buddies. The latter deeply in love newlyweds. Yet when one shares a home with another human being, as Simon so hilariously dramatizes, there is bound to be fights and friction.

Readers like strong identification. We relate to those who struggle. We identify with the woman who was not the May Queen. And the guy who was not Mr. Cool.

Woody Allen gets big laughs. He doesn't score with women (at least not in his early movies). There is nothing funny about Warren Beatty. He gets 'em every time.

Erma Bombeck is one of us. There is chaos in her home. Martha Stewart can probably make a centerpiece from pigeon droppings. Her gracious living is not funny.

People relate to floundering, not to breezing through life with ease. Humorists deal with their loser parts. With what they are missing or lacking. Their way is often self-degradation.

THE UNEXPECTED

Another thing that makes people laugh is the unexpected. The more surprising the better. Sid Caesar and his writers clearly proved that. So did Mike Nichols and Elaine May.

In *Metropolitan Life*, a collection of essays, Fran Leibowitz has surprising and irreverent things to say about mood jewelry, the art in Soho, houseplants, procrastination, children and so much more.

You must be willing to let go, make a fool of yourself, and trust the way you see it no matter how off-the-wall it is.

Six years ago I wrote an essay I sold to the *Times* Op-Ed page about male trial lawyers having more testosterone than other kinds of lawyers. I had read about a test done with saliva samples brought to a psychologist at Georgia State who kept them in mini spittoons in his freezer. When I read about this study in the newspaper one morning, I couldn't finish my coffee. My pen just started moving.

Here is my first paragraph of "Lawyers and Love, Hormonally Speaking":

> Life has changed for James M. Dabbs, Jr. since he started collecting saliva. By studying samples he keeps in mini spittoons in his freezer, Mr. Dabbs, a social psychologist at Georgia State University, has found that male trial lawyers have more testosterone than other kinds of lawyers. Not only is this information, which he presented at the American Psychological Society meeting in June, delighting male trial lawyers—it's inspiring people from around the country to send him their spit.

I had no idea I would get a whole essay out of it. I simply welcomed the opportunity to write about lawyers. Especially lawyers who spit. My sense of the ridiculous had truly been touched. A short time after I started this piece, a magazine editor spoke to my class. She happened to mention a study about another hormone: oxytocin. This sexual arousal hormone, findings showed, was the reason women want to connect to their men, while men want to connect to their boats.

So it was nothing we said or did then, I thought. It was the oxytocin.

Again I was perking. And giddy inside. As the editor continued talking to my students, I went on a little vacation from them and mentally took notes.

Oxytocin and testosterone. What if during the studies someone switched the hormone in the lab?

When I first started writing and even ten years ago, I wouldn't have trusted that glimmer in my eye. But I've learned to have fun viewing life—in this case hormones—in my own quirky way.

Surprising myself with what I have to say is one of the reasons I write. And until the *Times* bought that piece—and that didn't happen in a day—saying what I wanted about testosterone and oxytocin was more than enough. It was great.

Tips to Say It Funnier

1 Read *The New Yorker* and whoever's wit you admire. Woody Allen, Mark Twain and Dorothy Parker are required.

2 Write about whatever you find absurd. If something hits you, get it down.

3 Be simple. Be bold. Don't second-guess yourself. If it makes you giggle when you are alone, that is reason enough to say it.

4 You can get ideas from what you read and what you see at the movies or on television. From your family, romances and friends. From the conflicts and mishaps of your daily life. From the world outside your door.

More Specific Advice

1 Be brief. Humor is about brevity. Less is definitely more. Say it once. Pare it down. Pare it down some more. Jack Benny was a funny man. He hardly said a word.

2 Be direct. Cut through the clutter. Call a spade a spade.

CHAPTER THIRTY-FIVE

Rejections

When my sonnet was rejected, I exclaimed, "Damn the age:
I will write for antiquity."
        —*Charles Lamb*

I heard a voice on my answering machine one day that
sounded like death warmed over. It was an acquaintance—Ann, I'll call her—who was always telling me she
wrote. The last time I saw her, she had finished an essay she
wanted to send out. She thought she'd try the *Times*.

"Good idea," I had told her. "The *Times* is a great place to
start."

Now on my tape, Ann said she thought that I (who am neither
her best friend nor her pastor, mind you) should be the first to
know that the *Times* sent her their form rejection and she was a
total wreck. Her voice at first was like a 45 record on 33. Then
she was barely audible. My friends who've phoned in with malig-
nancies have sounded more upbeat.

Ann's final words right before hanging up were that she wasn't
sure she could cope.

"She might as well kill herself," said my daughter, who'd been listening along with me.

RULE NUMBER ONE: DON'T DESPAIR

Rejection letters have been a staple at our house. A regular part of our mail. I have probably gotten more "sorrys" than solicitations from the Fresh Air Fund.

Before I sold a single word, I collected 157 rejections. They were not for just one essay, but for the seven I was then shopping. With most, I followed my then-teacher's advice, which was to start with *The New Yorker*.

My first published effort, an essay about my college trip to Europe, had been to seventeen publications before it found a home. It was published in a magazine called *The Student*, which paid me twenty dollars. Figuring what I had spent on stamps and envelopes, I lost money on the deal.

On occasion, I almost lost the will to persevere. I remember one particular day. Four of my pieces were stuffed in my mailbox, all returned with form rejections. I burst into tears right there.

I stomped around my apartment. I cursed. I cried some more. Four "sorrys" in a single day was too much for one ego. There was no way I would ever write again. At least not for the marketplace.

Eventually, I called a published writer I knew and asked him for advice.

"Have you finished feeling sorry for yourself and calling all editors 'shits'?"

"No. Why?"

"When you do, type new title pages for the ones on which the editors left a coffee ring, then send them out again."

I did. Eventually two of the four were published. The other two ended up in my trunk.

I built up my immunity to rejection letters, but they don't

ever lose their sting. After the first few dozen, though, they become pricks and jabs and a matter of course, not long, teary afternoons.

RULE NUMBER TWO: KEEP SENDING YOUR WORK OUT

No one forces us to send our work out.

No one forces us to write.

If you want to see your work published, you have to keep pitching and persevere.

One of the pluses of a writing workshop is that others go through this same process. And it is a process.

After I'd been sending work out for a while, my mother asked how it was going.

"Really well," I told her. "I am getting better rejections."

There were stages. First came standard forms with phrases like, "Sorry it doesn't meet our needs" or "We don't accept unsolicited material."

Then at the top of these forms was "Dear Nancy."

Next, at the bottom was "try us again."

I invariably "tried them" while the iron was hot. This led to the next stage: personal rejections. Some were encouraging, more were not, but at least they were written by humans.

Sending work out for publication makes me think of a wonderful old Woody Allen line. When asked what fame has brought him, he says he gets turned down by a higher class of women.

If you want your work to be published, you have to deal with getting turned down. With some pieces, you may hit early. With others, not at all. Don't fall apart when you get those "nos." Don't fold up your tent.

When I told Ann, my acquaintance, the *Times* was a good place to start, I had not meant her career.

Advice

Retype the first page of your manuscript if the editor's coffee stains are on it and send it out again.

Further advice on rejection

Don't take rejection personally. There are any number of reasons why editors reject your work that have nothing to do with your writing. Three common ones: It doesn't fit their needs because of its tone, format, subject or intended audience, they just bought or ran something like it, or it simply did not wow them.

In the mid-eighties, I had an editor from *Parents* speak to my class. She brought in a half a dozen proposals she'd received for articles about AIDS. The one she accepted was a very personal story by a woman in New Jersey who found out a favorite neighbor had the AIDS virus. She had to share the news and explain it to her young son. Unlike the pieces the *Parents* editor had rejected, this had heart, specific details, a very clear focus and a voice. The others rambled, were didactic, too general, were missing that personal stamp or were perhaps lost to the editor's taste. And maybe, too, she was deluged with stories about AIDS.

Know the publications to which you are sending your work. This means knowing the audience, tone and format. The book *Writer's Market* has listings and descriptions, but you should carefully read the magazines and newspapers in which you would like your work to appear. Magazines have editorial guidelines they send to potential contributers on request. Reading these are not a substitute for really reading the magazine.

Send your work to the appropriate editor. Check the mastheads and send your work to a managing, senior or articles editor, not to the editor in chief unless your children are on the same soccer team, or you already have some connection. If you know or have met an editor, send it to that person.

Remember that editors move around. I submitted a piece to a new articles editor at *Redbook* that her predecessor had rejected. She bought it.

I think it is a good idea to send work to new editors, partly because they are looking to cultivate their own writers and also because they don't yet know what they want.

I've sold several pieces that had previously been rejected that way, including one to the *Times*.

Remember that when an editor rejects your work, it is just one person's opinion.

CHAPTER THIRTY-SIX

Don't Turn Your Friends and Loved Ones Into Critics

My relatives say that they are glad I'm rich, but that they simply cannot read me.

—Kurt Vonnegut, Jr.

My friend Elaine called me all excited. She is taking a writing class—her first—and just finished the first assignment. Her boyfriend, Joe, is going to read it later and since I am a "professional critiquer" she thought I might want to give her my opinion.

Elaine thought wrong. I told her so.

A short time before that my cousin Arnold had that very same thought. He had written a character sketch. Of me. The writing was OK. He explained way too much. Especially about my clutter.

I had told Arnold to cut and tighten. I actually used the words "clean up." And I used them quite emphatically about the parts where he called me a slob.

Our relationship has changed. So did two others—both with close friends—since I read their pieces. And neither was about me.

"But I'd *really* appreciate your honest opinion," Elaine now said (and probably thought).

"Show your work to your teacher and class, not to me or Joe."

That is My Honest Opinion.

For Elaine and now for you.

WHAT YOU'LL GET WHEN YOU ASK FOR "AN HONEST OPINION"

I understand the impulse to show the people you "hang with" your newer and more real self. We have all waved or wanted to wave our writing in the faces of loved ones. And as a writing teacher, I have, for many years and for many loved ones, been "the face."

Sharing your work with friends, family, the people who depend on you for their allowance and the person or people with whom you sleep may be hazardous to your writing, your ego and your relationships.

Why?

Having your work critiqued is more complicated than you think. Here are some possible scenarios:

When we ask our loved ones for an "honest opinion," that is not always what we want. Often when we say, "Tell me what you really think," we are *really* saying:

1. Please love it.
2. Please love me.
3. This is me. The real me. Aren't I touching and profound?
4. This is me. The real me. And I'm writing this so you will understand why I've been so totally out to lunch. Now you know about my

- serious drug problem
- break with the law
- break with reality
- abusive childhood
- therapist whom I like a whole lot better than you
- great disdain for you

Now even with opening one of the above cans of worms, your loved ones may be in awe of your talent. After all, these people like—even love—you and choose to be with you in person. Why shouldn't they like you in print?

OK. So now say you are pumped up with their wows and praise, but your writing class or editor isn't quite so knocked out. The teacher and other students say it needs more dialogue or more something. The editor sends it back.

Now you think one or more of the following:

- My husband (or friend) loved it. What does this editor know?
- My friend or my mate is brilliant. The teacher who hasn't published in ages is probably sour grapes.
- Why did I show my work to my loved ones? They coddle me. They're not professionals. What do they know?

If your loved ones like it, your ego and your writing may ride too much on their opinions. What if they don't like the next piece you show them? You wonder:

- Were they telling The Truth about the first?
- Maybe I can't really write.
- What do they know?

Now let us look at different scenarios:

Your loved ones do not like or get the piece you take to your class or send out for publication. The class loves it. The editor buys it.

You think:

- Why did I show it to my husband or my mother in the first place? They are hurt because I've exposed them. Or because I haven't written about them at all. They're jealous of my writing. Of my secrets. My new life.
- What do they know?
- Why didn't they understand? You get angry at their comments. Hurt because they don't really get your work. Or you.

A loved one's comments can hurt your work, your ego and your pride. If he doesn't like it, you may not be in such a hurry to write anything again.

Or . . . it can, subliminally or not so subliminally, put a distance or wedge between the two of you.

After all how can you hang out, live or sleep with someone who doesn't get the real you?

Advice

1 Don't show your writing to people in your life.

2 Find a group or class that is more objective, gentle, constructive, honest and supportive. As a veteran teacher and erstwhile student, I am a staunch believer in classes.

CHAPTER THIRTY-SEVEN

Writing Classes: Me as a Student

Let's go to work.
—*Quentin Tarantino*

My first three published efforts came out of the writing-class-I-took-for-several-semesters-and-not-because-I-flunked. I learned to write, not talk about it. I greatly improved my technique. My teacher was strict. A real grammar cop. And a totally terrific mentor. Had it not been for him, I'd still be working for New York's Board of Education. Probably as a guidance counselor.

But what I learned as a student was not just technique. I learned about the process and mindset for survival. I had discovered—am still discovering—a myriad of things about writing. About myself. And about selling.

MY FIRST PUBLISHED PIECE

I want to share what I arrived at with my earliest published pieces. The first was a children's story about a dog, Bently, who wanted to celebrate Halloween. My teacher had given me no suggested market list for this one, as he had for my others he'd deemed publishable. Nor had he given me encouragement or praise.

Nuh-uh. What he gave me instead was the distinct feeling that my "A Halloween Ride" made him puke.

He did not use the word "puke." He was too erudite, too well-bred and well schooled for that. He used the words "cloying" and "pathetic" to describe my plot, premise and dog, and the phrase "feeble attempt at humor" to describe my centerpiece scene in which Bently goes to a five-and-ten-cent store and tries on costumes.

He wasn't finished. Nope.

He announced to the entire class that among the serious literary efforts submitted the previous week was a "talking dog" story. Although he is not opposed to anthropomorphism, this particular story, which opens with the animal sitting in a comfortable chair and going to a store to try on costumes, was more than he could bear. If anyone planned on springing "talking animal" stories in the future, give him warning—ample warning—so he could at least try to mentally prepare. As he spoke the veins in his face popped out.

Fortunately, he did not read my story aloud. Nor did he reveal whose it was, but as he was talking my self-esteem went flying out the emergency exit. I shrivelled up. I was three inches tall.

I was one of the few people in the class writing for both adults and for children. Maybe this switching didn't work. Maybe my story was cloying. I was confused. Unsure of myself. And certainly clueless how to proceed. My renowned teacher—with his decades of experience and enormous following—obviously knows.

But . . . and it's a big one. Actually, it is two. And these two "buts" I'm about to share contradict an earlier stance.

My heart was in my dog story. I lived my premise. I loved the dog. I imbued him with traits that endear me to people: sincerity, individuality, compassion, feistiness and humanity. I made Bently a loyal friend, a contemplative soul and a downright spirited companion.

Intent to work on the story and make it as good as I could, I revised it several times, and without showing it to my teacher again, I sent it out. It was published the following October.

In a previous section, I rebuked my students who aren't open to suggestions. I still feel one should be open. Being open to what does and doesn't work enables writers to grow. We are often too close to the process. Detached and trusted opinions help.

As a writer, I was open to my teacher's suggestions. With editors now, I still am. But everyone has quirks, different tastes, aversions and pet peeves. And my writing teacher had a strong disdain for animal stories and was not innately sensitive to their charms.

My stronger feelings for that work ultimately willed out. I was compelled to tell that story. I believed someone out there might say "yes."

Even teachers like me and like mine are not right about everything.

Listen to so-called voices of authority, but ultimately do as you wish.

EGREGIOUSLY LIBERATING

My teacher had scared me the first night. He was high-minded, widely published and tall. If that didn't send me to the "drop" and "add" office that first half hour, his opening remarks almost did. He used the word "egregious" to describe the kind of error we would be making if we didn't make writing a regular thing.

Oy!

As soon as I figured out what "egregious" meant, I realized that was why I was there. To have someone tell me to get with the program and sit my fanny down. Did it matter that he was not someone who could be my closest personal friend?

I didn't know.

Two things happened the next hour that set my wheels in motion. First, he gave us our home assignment: the two-page character sketch of someone we knew well who has gotten under our skin. My pen started moving as he spoke. I was getting my then mother-in-law down.

The teacher went on. "It has to be someone you feel strongly about."

I had my mother-in-law rearranging my furniture. As the teacher continued, I was going to it, writing about The General in her mink.

I saw the possibilities. Of writing freely and having fun. The teacher may be a card-carrying intellect, but thou's and tis's weren't his thing.

And then he turned me on to Dorothy Parker. He spent the rest of the first session reading excerpts from her stories and sharing her best retorts, waxing poetic about both her writing and her wit.

His Dorothy Parker penchant was liberating. I could write about what tickled me, about what I found absurd. With the sketch about my mother-in-law, I started to let go.

THE BENEFITS

What other benefits did I reap from that class?

I had a place to now take my work. I began developing discipline. The more I wrote, the more feedback I got. And I wanted feedback. It "came with."

It was a chicken and egg thing, really. I'm not sure whether I took the course because I was ready to write, or made the commitment to do it because I was there. What I do know is that when I put down money, I want a return.

Years later I went to the first meeting of Smokenders and as I wrote them a check, I knew I would quit smoking. They could have shown me Marx Brothers movies for the next six weeks rather than put me through behavioral modification. My commitment to stop was there. The same was true when I joined a health club. There'd be no whenever-I-can-get-there deal. It would be push and pull and sweat and squat three to six times a week.

Subliminally I knew when I paid the writing course fee that the teacher's personality and expectations wouldn't matter. I would grab everything I could.

Which I did. I wrote regularly. Got my teacher's feedback. Had a place where I showed up. And a group.

I liked being around people who were doing the same thing. It made me feel less lonely. Before that I'd never known anyone who wrote or wanted to write. It was a supportive, encouraging environment.

The woman whom I sat with became a friend outside of class. We phoned each other and regularly had coffee. She was the person to whom I turned when I was about to quit teaching to write full time.

"I'm afraid I'll have nothing to write about," I told her.

I can still hear her response. "Your second graders didn't make you a writer. You'll see it your way wherever you are."

THE SECOND TIME AROUND

My second published work, "An Apple for My Children," was an essay about taking a fifth grade class—not my own—to the Museum of Natural History. Their teacher was absent. Their sub had a heart problem and according to the principal was "too weak to handle such monsters." So the sub had my class. I took the field trip and got a migraine and an essay from it.

The first draft I handed into class was more than fifteen pages. The one I sold to *Learning Magazine* was a paragraph under five. Between the two were several drafts. I pruned and tightened and cut.

That was my first experience with cleaning up clutter and

boiling my work down to its essence. I learned with "An Apple for My Children" that *most writing is about revision.*

BEYOND *THE NEW YORKER*

My third published piece also came out of that class and it was about my first trip to Europe. My teacher suggested five publications beginning with *The New Yorker.* When *The New Yorker* rejected it, I sent it to the other four. The others wrote "no" so I kept going with a list I made myself. My "Travels With a Novice" went out seventeen times before it found a home.

I was one of the few people from that class who went on to have work published regularly. And not because I was the best writer. There were much better writers in that class with me. They bagged it when *The New Yorker* wrote "no."

Exercise

Think of a teacher who changed your life for better or for worse. What was it about the person or teaching that touched you? How did you change? Write about your experience with that teacher and class and how it shaped your life.

CHAPTER THIRTY-EIGHT

Getting the Most From Writing Classes

It was here, in this noisome place, in spite of all I had read and been taught and thought I knew about it before, that the mysterious, awful power of writing first dawned on me.

—*Elizabeth Bishop*

Dave, a newish student in my advanced workshop, walked in one evening kvetching. He had been re-working an essay using our suggestions, and was getting fed up with revising.

Tough I wanted to tell him, but I'm a professional. That wouldn't be cool. So I said what is often the smartest thing to say. Absolutely nothing.

Dave read Draft Three. He had made good changes. It was stronger than Drafts One and Two. We pointed out how it could be better still, making suggestions for Draft Four.

"Again?" Dave mumbled.

"At least," said a veteran reviser.

Basic training in a writing class should be learning to revise.

We had seen fourteen drafts of Michele's shrink piece (discussed in an earlier chapter) before she sent it to the *Times*. She's motivated, likes revising and has the hang of hanging in. Like other committed students, she does major surgery, moves paragraphs around, fleshes out, goes deeper and tweaks.

A teacher can't teach you to write as much as give you what you need to revise. I've seen amazing growth in my students' writing. They've traveled far since they first walked in.

Would they have become as good without the class?

That I really can't say.

I do think writing classes can help in the following ways:

1. **You have a place to show up regularly with your writing.**

    I tell my students at the first session I get paid regardless of what they bring. I will still entertain them if they come empty-handed. My class is a fun evening out.

    But if they are anything like me—I hope they and you are too—you want as much feedback as possible to see how to best revise.

    Taking a class gets you in the groove. You begin developing disciplined habits. You write regularly. Bring work in. Learn how to make it better.

    When I do my job right and my students do theirs, I become like the Weight Watchers Lady. I am the person who checks or weighs them in, validating their at-home labors.

2. **You are most inclined to give it your all if you make a monetary investment.**

    Everything has a price. Nothing worthwhile is free. I strongly believe most people stay with it if they pay a required course fee.

    When I took an aerobics class for AIDS, which required a contribution, I bounced a lot harder and sweated much more than when I bounced and sweated for free.

It's human nature to want a return for our money.

We want and should take what "comes with."

A writing class is a great investment of your money and yourself.

3. You have your own editorial staff.

You have a new built-in group offering feedback. It's not loaded as it might be at home. Hopefully, the criticism is honest and constructive. And hopefully, you use it well.

You will learn, if you stay with it, how different people critique. Some respond from the gut. Some from the head. Some are general and see the whole picture. Some are very specific with advice about words and little details. The lawyers and teachers in the group will niggle and pick. And pick.

The minister in my advanced workshop looks for the big "aha."

I think a wide range of responses is useful to the writer. You get to see your work from all angles. Understand where each person's comments come from. Be open. Take it all in.

Then use whatever feels right. Ultimately, your work is yours.

4. You feel less lonely.

Writing is a lonely pursuit. We physically isolate ourselves. And if we dig and probe and go deeply within, it can be scary coming back.

It is comforting to touch base with like-minded souls on similar paths. They understand what you go through. The empathy and shared experience help when you hit snags, get rejections or even need a new spin.

5. It can be stimulating, exciting and inspiring.

When my student Lou finished his second novel, we celebrated after class by going out. Hannah, who'd been there since Lou began his first, was literally getting chills.

In my class, whenever anyone breaks new ground, revises

something until it sings, or finishes or publishes an essay or story or book we'd seen at all stages, the others invariably rejoice.

It's like being on the same team.

The stronger writers pull the others up. When someone is stuck, another helps. My student Jane, who has trouble with dialogue, picks my best dialogue writers' brains. Jane's ear is developing. Her dialogue has improved. More often now it rings true.

You inspire each other in how you say it. And also in what you say. You get ideas from another student's work. A good class is very alive.

Advice on What to Look for in a Class

Read the course description in the catalog carefully to make sure it's what you want. Make sure, too, that whatever else is happening you will be writing regularly and bringing your work in.

Check the teacher's credentials. See who the teacher is. Was she highly recommended? Does she get the kind of writing you want to do?

Find someone with the right mix of toughness and tenderness. Who makes you work, but offers support. She should know your strengths and weaknesses, and be able to show you ways to improve.

If you are not comfortable with a teacher for whatever reason, you may not be comfortable on the page.

CHAPTER THIRTY-NINE

Will You Hold for the Editor in Chief?

My definition of a good editor is a man I think charming,
who sends me large checks, praises my work, my physical
beauty, my sexual prowess, and who has a stranglehold on
the publisher and the bank.

—*John Cheever*

Waiting For Daddy," which I previously discussed, was the first piece I submitted to *Parents*. An editor there, who was a friend of a friend, mentioned they were looking for personal essays.

My piece was personal. Very personal. And not what one might call "upbeat." Part of me was afraid to show them my serious, sad side first. The larger part took over though and said, "Send it. What the hell?"

They bought my despair. They liked my wallowing. The editor called with the news and my fee. It was my largest writing fee to date. And it would go up, she even mentioned, if I wanted to wallow again.

I was jubilant. And rejoicing. It was "Onward Christian Soldiers" now. I could continue to write what was in my heart. *Parents* would give me space.

A week after this verbal acceptance, I got a call from the secretary of the editor in chief. "She'd like to have a word with you," the secretary said. "Would you hold while I put her on?"

My stomach dropped. Obviously, they made a mistake. Or changed their minds. Or accepted my work without her approval. It was a classy move, on her part though, to be the one to deal the blow.

"Nancy Kelton, Nancy Kelton," said the editor in chief without a hello. "Have you written for us before?"

"No," I said and that was it, figuring less is more.

"I know your name though. How?"

"Probably my *Times* pieces," I quickly said, always eager to give them a plug.

"That's not it."

For several seconds I did not speak, then quietly, very quietly, I told her, "I think I sent you some work before."

"Aren't you sure?"

I gulped. "I did."

"Here?"

"No, when you were the articles editor at *New York*."

There were several seconds of silence, then she said, "Right." She paused again—to give me a moment for my coronary. "You sent a lot to me at *New York*, didn't you?"

Oh boy! "Ten article proposals," I quietly squeaked out.

"Yes! Yes!" she wasn't having an orgasm, I don't think, but it all was coming back. "That's great!"

"Great?"

"You obviously have a lot to say."

Nothing came out of my mouth.

She went on. "So I know you're in it for the long haul."

I was. Still am today.

FIVE TIPS FOR WRITING AND MARKETING

1. Write what you really feel. If you reach deep enough inside yourself, you will reach other people too.
2. Study the markets. Know the contents, tone, format and audience of the magazines you target. Editors like to think you've done your homework and know what their publications are about.
3. Study the mastheads. Editors move. Each has her own vision, taste, agenda, likes. What works for one doesn't necessarily work for the next. And what fits in at one publication may not fit in at another.
4. Be persistent. In marketing (in everything) that's key. I was praised and rewarded for sending ten proposals that didn't make it. With number eleven, I hit.
5. It only takes one.

EPILOGUE

I had planned on ending this book by returning to my favorite theme—that good writing takes courage, a willingness to let people see your insides, discipline and fierce determination.

But how can I return to something I never really left?

I had also planned on reminding you

- to let the words come pouring out.
- not to second-guess yourself.
- that your experiences needn't be traumatic or side-splitting.
- that your revelations are what matters.

So I just did.

Which is what I have been doing all along. I hope you practice what I've preached.

I hope, too, that you write because, like me, you think the printed word is "It." Capable of hitting all the right notes, capturing our common humanity and touching us at the core.

Mostly though, I hope you write because you want to write. First, foremost and always for and from yourself.

Not for approval.

Or fame.

Or money.

Or for anything that comes from outside.

And certainly not for the stroking or visibility you didn't get from mom.

I grew up in a house in which there was great respect for the word. And humorists got the last one. So it is only fitting that I give them the last words here.

On a recent PBS Special about Sid Caesar's "Your Show of Shows," one of the writers told a story about the time he brought his mother there. After watching the first sketch, he asked her what she thought.

"That Caesar is amazing," she said.

"Ma, I worked on that sketch," the writer told her.

She went on. "What a talent Caesar is!"

In the next sketch, Sid used several different languages. When it was over, the writer's mother was again in awe.

"That man," she said. "There is no end to his talent."

"I wrote that sketch," the son told her.

But she wasn't done. "Caesar can make jokes. He can do languages. A fabulous talent."

The next sketch was a musical number. Same thing.

"Look at how he dances and sings," said the mother.

"I wrote that one, too, Ma."

"That guy Caeser can do anything," said the mother.

It went on like that for the entire show. When it was over, the writer went backstage to tell Sid what a great job he did and to share the story about his mother.

Sid listened. "You know," he said, "my mother was here just a few minutes ago, too. I asked her what she thought of the show. You know what she said? She said, 'Boy, you must have *some* writers.' "

The following parts of the appendix offer a case study, of sorts, showing how I published a personal experience piece titled "Waiting for Daddy." I sent the piece, along with the cover letter in part one, to Wendy Schuman, an editor at *Parents* magazine. Another editor at the magazine, Elizabeth Crow, read the piece and bought it. You'll find her comments in part three. In part two you'll find the piece itself. Notice in the cover letter that the original title was "The Friday Night Exchange."

APPENDIX—PART ONE

Cover Letter to *Parents*

October 3, 1982

Wendy Schuman-Senior Editor
Parents
685 Third Avenue
New York, New York 10017

Dear Wendy:

Enclosed please find my piece, "The Friday Night Exchange." I hope you find it suitable for publication.

I am the author of four children's books and numerous magazine pieces. I am enclosing copies of my published work from The *Times*, *Learning* and *Glamour*.

Thank you for your kind consideration.

Sincerely yours,

Nancy Kelton

Notes on the cover letter:

1. If the editor in chief is not a relative, bedpartner, friend or close acquaintance, send your manuscript to the articles, managing or senior editor. Use the person's name. If you know an editor or anyone else on the staff, by all means use your contacts.

2. If you have published credits, say so in your letter and enclose clips of your work. If you don't, a few sentences stating you are enclosing a piece, hope it's suitable and appreciate the attention are enough.

APPENDIX—PART TWO

Waiting for Daddy

BY NANCY KELTON

It's six o'clock on Friday—a warm, spring Friday evening. I just finished packing my five-year-old daughter Emily's overnight bag and she is now putting in her favorite stuffed animal and her new fruit-flavored lip balm. Her father is coming to pick her up for their weekend visit and she wants to wait outside where Jamie and Katy, her friends from the building, are trying out Jamie's new bike.

As we ride down in the elevator, Emily bends down to play with a wirehaired terrier and proceeds to tell its owner that at home she has no pets but at her Dad's she has goldfish. I listen to the matter-of-factness and ease with which she discusses her two parents' homes as if it were as commonplace as having two eyes or two ears, and I feel an enormous wave of emotions swelling up inside me.

We've come a long way, he and I, a long way, indeed. I remember the first Saturday he came for her after we'd separated, almost two years ago. At first there was an icy silence and then as he and I attempted to discuss the logistics of Emily's first sleepover at his new apartment, all our raw pain and anger spilled out in an exchange of caustic remarks that escalated into the hurling of harsh, ugly words. Emily reacted to the confusion in which we were floundering by crying that she didn't want to go. She clung to me for security, but my efforts to reassure her that everything was okay only fueled her tantrum, because my voice and body told her otherwise. As I stood at the door of the apartment watching him carry out our child, then barely three, I broke down weeping as I had never wept before.

Little by little I learned to survive these weekend exchanges along with the other aspects of my new life, constantly reminding myself of the advice of a close friend who also happens to be a divorced parent. "The pain never vanishes," he said, "so you'll have to start moving and working with it."

The elevator door opens at the lobby. Our play date with Jamie's bike doesn't look so promising—Jamie and Katy are coming toward us, followed by their mother and their father with his briefcase, just home from work. They have to go up now. It's time for supper. My daughter and I stand in silence watching the elevator door close. I wonder if she's just disappointed that her friends can no longer play or if she's feeling pangs similar to mine, picturing the four members of this tight unit riding up together to share a family meal.

I felt the same sort of pang a few Saturdays ago. Emily was at her father's and I was taking a walk with Alan, the man I have been seeing for the past year, when I saw a family I knew leaving the park, each parent carrying a sleeping child.

"They're such a happy family," I said, staring longingly.

"You're a happy family, too. You and Emily," said Alan.

He was right. Most of the time Emily and I are a happy family. But there are certain occasions, like holidays and school functions and moments like these, when I am confronted with a happy, intact family, or at least the image of one, and suddenly it hits me hard—very, very hard—that something important is missing from our lives and we are not a happy family at all but a rather skimpy one.

Alan continued, "And when you include me, we're all a happy family."

His words touched me deeply. What he said was true: with the exception of those very special moments I have shared alone with my daughter, some of the warmest moments of my entire life have been with Emily and Alan together. How bittersweet it is that this man who rounds out our family picture so beautifully is not the father of my child.

A voice from outside calls to Emily. It belongs to a girl of about nine from the neighborhood who often plays in front of our building. Today she's jumping rope. Emily wants to try. I follow her out with the overnight bag.

"Where are you going?" the girl asks me.

"Nowhere," I tell her. "Emily's going to her father's."

"You mean you don't live together?" she says.

"That's right."

"Are you separated or something?"

"Uh huh."

From Sixth Avenue I see him coming toward us with his attaché case in one hand and his folded up *Times* in the other. For a second—a brief second—it feels as if he is coming home.

The girl continues, "Is that him?"

I nod. Her questions are beginning to annoy me. So is the way she studies him. Is she wondering why and when we stopped loving each other? Or is she thinking how sad it must be for all of us that we cannot be together?

As he joins our little group, he bends over to kiss Emily and then acknowledges me with a polite hello.

"Are you going to get divorced?" the girl asks me.

"Yes," I say, flashing him a forced smile and then looking over at Emily, who is oblivious, or pretending to be oblivious, of the conversation.

"Who's your friend?" he asks.

I'm not sure whether he's addressing me or Emily, but I feel compelled to answer. "A girl from the neighborhood who asks a lot of questions."

The edge in my voice makes her back off a few feet. Emily follows.

We stand there alone, he and I, his eyes carefully avoiding mine. I remind him that Emily has a birthday party on Sunday and he asks if I packed her shorts, because he's taking her on a picnic tomorrow. I glance at him watching Emily trying to get both feet over the rope at the same time. She can't quite do it, but she keeps at it. There's such softness in his face. It always came through for her.

The girl from the neighborhood has to leave. Emily reluctantly gives her back the rope and then comes and stands between the two of us, looking from me to her father and back at me again, waiting to see what will happen next.

"I wish I could jump rope," she says, breaking our tense silence. "I really do."

The earnestness in her voice makes me wonder what she's really asking for, but I don't want to pursue it. Not now. We've dawdled long enough.

"Have a great weekend, sweetie pie," I say, giving her a big hug and kiss.

She hugs and kisses me back and then skips ahead to the girl for one last attempt with the jump rope. As her father follows with her overnight bag, I feel that familiar lump in my throat—a lump that, unlike my tears or anger, I cannot stop from forming whenever we play this scene.

APPENDIX—PART THREE

Elizabeth Crow's Response

The minute I read "Waiting for Daddy," I knew Nancy Kelton is the Real Thing—a writer who can describe tough emotional experiences without falling into any of the traps that seduce a lot of less talented writers. Here's what I mean: Nancy didn't write "Waiting for Daddy" for any of the usual reasons: to get back at her ex-husband, or to elicit pity for her situation, or to pursue any agenda other than to describe a setting and a situation— and the people in a homely little domestic drama—as simply and truthfully as possible. The result of this straightforward approach was miraculous. There were no barriers between her and the reader, who felt invited, metaphorically at least, to put on Nancy's shoes and walk around in them for a few minutes. I identified with Nancy. I could feel the late afternoon city heat on my shoulders. I could feel her ambivalence about letting her daughter out of her sight for a weekend. I could feel her fear, her loneliness and, above all, her strength and honesty. It was there explicitly and implicitly.

In this short essay, Nancy made me her friend and ally— without making me feel manipulated (as in, Mom is good; Dad is Yuppie Scum). She described her daughter's interactions with older children in front of her building in a way that both reassured the reader that Emily was all right (very important for the anxious new parents who read *Parents* magazine). And, as important, helped the reader identify with Nancy's wistfulness about the family she didn't have, without ever resorting to the kind of hanky-twisting agony-prose that can be offputting and annoying to readers. I look for writers who tell the truth, who can give readers hope that they, too, can not just survive life's tough situations but triumph, given a little humor, a little candor and a hefty dose of realism.

Writers who want to tell their own stories are lucky: They've lived interesting lives and they think there's some meaning for others in their experiences. There probably is—but the reader is only likely to glean this meaning if the writer is skillful. Here are the qualities I look for in a first-person article:

1. **Keep it simple.**

I want a story that is told clearly and directly. Hold the histrionics. I'm more likely to laugh or cry—whichever the author intended—if I'm disarmed by the writer's candor. And I'm likely to be as unmoved as a stone if I know that I'm being manipulated.

2. **Respect the reader.**

Let me decide who are the story's villains and heroes. I don't need to have characters' motives and darkest deeds characterized. I can get the picture from seeing them in action, from hearing them speak. I can feel the passion and enthusiasm and affection or scorn in a good writer's voice without having to have these emotions explained to me.

3. **Look for meaning.**

Every good story has a point. If a personal experience is told honestly and with passion (but without theatrics), it will have strength, and it will have meaning. It will touch me because it's truthful. And if the lessons the writer or her subject learned are clear to me—without being preached to me—I'll be a smarter, wiser and maybe even a better person as a result.

(Elizabeth Crow purchased "Waiting for Daddy" while editor at *Parents*. She is now editor in chief at *Mademoiselle*.)

INDEX

More Great Books for Writers!

Elements of the Writing Craft—Apply the techniques of the masters in your own work! This collection of 150 lessons reveals how noted writers have "built" their fiction and nonfiction. Each exercise contains a short passage of work from a distinguished writer, a writer's-eye analysis of the passage and a wealth of innovative writing exercises. *#48027/$19.99/272 pages*

Writer's Digest Handbook of Making Money Freelance Writing— Discover promising new income-producing opportunities with this collection of articles by top writers, editors and agents. Over 30 commentaries on business issues, writing opportunities and freelancing will help you make the break to a full-time writing career. *#10501/$19.99/320 pages*

1,818 Ways to Write Better & Get Published—If you need to know it, use it, act on it, it's here—in easy-to-search, fast-reference form. Handy checklists detail everything from how to name characters and overcome writer's block to what business contacts can do for writers. *#10508/$12.99/224 pages/paperback*

Writing Personal Essays—Discover how to put your life story on paper. You'll learn how to choose just the right personal-experience topic and how to build a story loaded with emotion and significance. Bender offers inspiration to help you every step of the way. *#10438/$17.99/272 pages/paperback*

Writing Articles From the Heart: How to Write & Sell Your Life Experiences— Holmes gives you heartfelt advice and inspiration on how to get your personal essay onto the page. You'll discover how to craft a story to meet your needs and those of your readers. *#10352/$16.99/176 pages*

The Writer's Digest Dictionary of Concise Writing—Make your work leaner, crisper and clearer! Under the guidance of professional editor Robert Hartwell Fiske, you'll learn how to rid your work of common say-nothing phrases while making it tighter and easier to read and understand. *#10482/$19.99/352 pages*

How to Write Attention-Grabbing Query & Cover Letters—Use the secrets Wood reveals to write queries perfectly tailored, too good to turn down! In this guidebook, you will discover why boldness beats blandness in queries every time, ten basics you *must* have in your article queries, ten query blunders that can destroy publication chances and much more. *#10462/$17.99/208 pages*

Discovering the Writer Within: 40 Days to More Imaginative Writing—Uncover the creative individual inside who will, with encouragement, turn secret thoughts and special moments into enduring words. You'll learn how to find something exciting in unremarkable places, write punchy first sentences for imaginary stories, give a voice to inanimate objects and much more! *#10472/$14.99/192 pages/paperback*

1999 Novel & Short Story Writer's Market—Get the information you need to get your short stories and novels published. You'll discover 2,000+ listings on fiction publishers, plus original articles on fiction writing techniques; detailed subject categories to help you target appropriate publishers; and interviews with writers, publishers and editors! *#10581/$22.99/656 pages*

The 30-Minute Writer—Write short, snappy articles that make editors sit up and take notice. Full-time freelancer Connie Emerson reveals the many types of quickly written articles you can sell—from miniprofiles and one-pagers to personal essays. You'll also learn how to match your work to the market as you explore methods for expanding from short articles to columns, and even books! *#10489/$14.99/256 pages/paperback*

Writing to Sell, Fourth Edition—You'll discover high-quality writing and marketing counsel in this classic writing guide from well-known agent Scott Meredith. His timeless advice will guide you along the professional writing path as you get help with creating characters, plotting a novel, placing your work, formatting a manuscript, deciphering a publishing contract—even combating a slump! *#10476/$17.99/240 pages*

Writer's Encyclopedia, Third Edition—Rediscover this popular writer's reference— now with information about electronic resources, plus more than 100 new entries. You'll find facts, figures, definitions and examples designed to answer questions about every discipline connected with writing and help you convey a professional image. *#10464/$22.99/560 pages/62 b&w illus.*

Writing and Selling Your Novel—Write publishable fiction from start to finish with expert advice from professional novelist Jack Bickham! You'll learn how to develop effective work habits, refine your fiction writing technique, and revise and tailor your novels for tightly targeted markets. *#10509/$17.99/208 pages*

The Writer's Digest Handbook of Short Story Writing, Volume II—Orson Scott Card, Dwight V. Swain, Kit Reed and other noted authors bring you sound advice and timeless techniques for every aspect of the writing process. *#10239/$13.99/252 pages/paperback*

The Writer's Legal Guide, Revised Edition—Now the answer to all your legal questions is right at your fingertips! The updated version of this treasured desktop companion contains essential information on business issues, copyright protection and registration, contract negotiation, income taxation, electronic rights and much, much more. *#10478/$19.95/256 pages/paperback*

The Writer's Digest Sourcebook for Building Believable Characters—Create unforgettable characters as you "attend" a roundtable where six novelists reveal their approaches to characterization. You'll probe your characters' backgrounds, beliefs and desires with a fill-in-the-blanks questionnaire. And a thesaurus of characteristics will help you develop the many other features no character should be without. *#10463/$17.99/288 pages*

The Writer's Guide to Everyday Life in Renaissance England—Give your readers a new view of Renaissance England, brimming with the details of daily life. With this one-of-a-kind reference you'll discover a world of facts—from fashions and courtship, to life in the Royal Court and religious festivals. *#10484/$18.99/272 pages/20 b&w illus.*

Get That Novel Written: From Initial Idea to Final Edit—Take your novel from the starting line to a fabulous finish! Professional writer Donna Levin shows you both the basics and the finer points of novel writing while you learn to use words with precision, create juicy conflicts, master point of view and more! *#10481/$18.99/208 pages*

20 Master Plots (And How to Build Them)—Write great contemporary fiction from timeless plots. This guide outlines 20 plots from various genres and illustrates how to adapt them into your own fiction. *#10366/$17.99/240 pages*

Description—Discover how to use detailed description to awaken the reader's senses; advance the story using only relevant description; create original word depictions of people, animals, places, weather and much more! *#10451/$15.99/176 pages*

Amateur Detectives: A Writer's Guide to How Private Citizens Solve Criminal Cases—Make your amateur-crime-solver novels and stories accurate and convincing! You'll investigate what jobs work well with sleuthing, information-gathering methods, the law as it relates to amateur investigators and more! *#10487/$16.99/240 pages/paperback*

Writing the Short Story: A Hands-On Writing Program—With Jack Bickham's unique "workshop on paper" you'll plan, organize, write, revise and polish a short story. Clear instruction, helpful charts and practical exercises will lead you every step of the way! *#10421/$16.99/224 pages*

Travel Writing: A Guide to Research, Writing and Selling—Bring your travels home in print as you discover the many types of articles there are to write—and how to do it. You'll learn how to make your journey into a salable article by finding information, verifying it and bringing it to life on paper. *#10465/$18.99/256 pages*

Aliens and Alien Societies—Gain a better understanding of extraterrestrial life to develop viable creatures and cultures using this fascinating reference. You'll have science on your side as you uncover the secrets of biochemistry, engineering and space travel. Plus, you'll learn to portray aliens as individuals true to their species. *#10469/$17.99/240 pages*

Romance Writer's Sourcebook: Where to Sell Your Manuscripts—Get your romance manuscripts published with this new resource guide that combines how-to-write instruction with where-to-sell direction. You'll uncover advice from established authors, as well as detailed listings of publishing houses, agents, organizations, contests and more! *#10456/$19.99/475 pages*

The Writer's Digest Guide to Manuscript Formats—Don't take chances with your hard work! Learn how to prepare and submit books, poems, scripts, stories and more with the professional look editors expect from a good writer. *#10025/$19.99/200 pages*

Science Fiction and Fantasy Writer's Sourcebook, 2nd Edition—Discover how to write and sell your science fiction and fantasy! Novel excerpts, short stories and advice from pros show you how to write a winner! Then over 300 market listings bring you publishers hungry for your work! Plus, you'll get details on SF conventions, online services, organizations and workshops. *#10491/$19.99/480 pages*

Writing and Illustrating Children's Books for Publication: Two Perspectives—Discover how to create a good, publishable manuscript in only eight weeks! You'll cover the writing process in its entirety—from generating ideas and getting started, to submitting a manuscript. Imaginative writing and illustrating exercises build on these lessons and provide fuel for your creative fires! *#10448/$24.95/128 pages*

The Art and Craft of Novel Writing—Using examples from classic and contemporary writers ranging from John Steinbeck to Joyce Carol Oates, Oakley Hall guides you through the process of crafting a novel. In example-packed discussions, Hall shows what works and why. *#48002/$14.99/240 pages/paperback*

The Writer's Digest Character Naming Sourcebook—Forget the guesswork! Twenty thousand first and last names (and their meanings!) from around the world will help you pick the perfect name to reflect your character's role, place in history and ethnicity. *#10390/$18.99/352 pages*